NUTSHELLS

EMPLOYMENT LAW
IN A NUTSHELL

AUSTRALIA
Law Book Co.
Sydney

CANADA and USA
Carswell
Toronto

HONG KONG
Sweet & Maxwell Asia

NEW ZEALAND
Brookers
Wellington

SINGAPORE and MALAYSIA
Sweet & Maxwell Asia
Singapore and Kuala Lumpur

NUTSHELLS

EMPLOYMENT LAW IN A NUTSHELL

SECOND EDITION

by

Andrew C. Bell
Lecturer in Law at Nottingham Trent University

London • Sweet & Maxwell • 2003

First Edition 2001
Second Edition 2003
Reprinted 2004

Published by Sweet & Maxwell Limited of
100 Avenue Road, Swiss Cottage, London NW3 3PF
http://www.sweetandmaxwell.co.uk
Computerset by
LBJ Typesetting Ltd of Kingsclere
Printed by Creative Print & Design, Wales

No natural forests were destroyed to make this product:
only farmed timber was used and replanted

ISBN 0 421 78370 2

**A CIP catalogue record for this book
is available from the British Library**

344.01
T27CR0

CONTENTS

ABBREVIATIONS

ACAS	—Advisory, Conciliation and Arbitration Service
CCT	—Compulsory Competitive Tendering
CRE	—Commission for Racial Equality
DDA	—Disability Discrimination Act 1995
EA	—Employment Act 2002
EAT	—Employment Appeals Tribunal
ECHR	—European Court of Human Rights
ECJ	—European Court of Justice
EDT	—Effective Date of Termination
EOC	—Equal Opportunities Commission
ERA	—Employment Rights Act 1996
ERelA	—Employment Relations Act 1999
EqPA	—Equal Pay Act 1970
ETO	—Economic Technical or Organisational (reason)
GOQ	—Genuine Occupational Qualification
HRA	—Human Rights Act 1998
HSE	—Health and Safety Executive
HSWA	—Health and Safety at Work Act 1974
NMWA	—National Minimum Wage Act 1998
PIDA	—Public Interest Disclosure Act 1998
RRA	—Race Relations Act 1976
SDA	—Sex Discrimination Act 1975
SI	—Statutory Instrument
SOSR	—Some Other Substantial Reason
TULR(C)A	—Trade Union and Labour Relations (Consolidation) Act 1992
TUPE	—Transfer of Undertakings (Protection of Employment) Regulations 1981

INTRODUCTION

This book is designed as a revision guide, not as a textbook. It covers not only individual employment law—that is the relationship between the employer and the employee—but also collective labour law, the relationships between the individual employee and the trade union, and the trade union and the employer.

You should be aware that Employment Law is dynamic, it does not stand still, and it is constantly being updated and revised.

You must ensure that you keep up to date with developments, new statutes, domestic caselaw and opinions of the European Court of Justice (ECJ); most of which will appear in the specialist journals and newsletters. It is also a good idea to get into the habit of regularly reading a non-sensationalist national daily newspaper; cases are often reported in the body of a newspaper long before they reach the law reports.

It is important that you should view Employment Law not as a "black letter law" subject, but in its social context. Until forty or fifty years ago there was relatively little legislation controlling the employment relationship, the government had traditionally adopted a *laissez faire* approach, regarding employment as a matter for the employer and employee to arrange within a very broad or loose legislative framework. The increase in power of the trade unions, a growing social awareness and an increase both in industrial disputes and media coverage of them throughout the 1960s and 1970s, focused the attention of both the public and the government on reform. The reform was aimed at the relationship of the parties in an employment context; no longer just the employer and employee, but now the government, the trade unions, the employer and the employee.

Britain's joining of the European Union helped focus attention on the "rights of workers", and the government, particularly Mrs Thatcher's government of the 1980s, used the opportunity to severely reduce the power of the unions, whilst creating or codifying an individual floor of rights; thus moving the emphasis from the collective to the individual.

Although the present Labour government has introduced legislation regarding union recognition, it seems unlikely that there will be any appreciable move away from the emphasis on the individual worker, and any return to the unions of their power and influence of the 1970s looks very doubtful.

Although much Employment Law is now consolidated into statute, the interpretation of that statute and some other areas of the law rely heavily on case law. During the course of your studies you will be referred to—and hopefully read—hundreds of cases from tribunal decisions to ECJ opinions. It is hardly realistic to expect either that you remember all of these cases, or that all of them can be included in a book such as this.

As you know, to a lawyer the importance of case law is not in the facts of the case as such, but in the legal principle and the use of the case as authority to support (or perhaps argue against) that particular principle. The facts of cases can, however, be important to you as a student—both in order to help you to remember and identify the case, and also as an example or explanation of the principle it follows or proves.

You should be familiar with most of the case law used in this book—if you are not you could either substitute a similar case with which you are familiar, or read the facts of the case, either in its original in the law report, or in precis form from one of the case books presently on the market.

In Employment Law examinations it is often the case that your final answer is of less importance than the way by which you arrived at it; in other words your legal argument supported by statute and case law will almost certainly gain you more marks than your conclusion.

Finally, remember that knowledge and understanding are two very different things; knowledge without the ability to apply it to any given situation will avail you of very little, whilst understanding is not possible without first gaining the knowledge. To be successful you will need both—Good Luck!

1. SOURCES OF EMPLOYMENT LAW

All of your authorities to support any proposition in Employment Law will be either statute or case law, and often a
combination of both. It is therefore important that you should
understand the sources of these authorities and the relationship
between them.

It may be said that there are three main sources of Employment Law in this country:

Statute

The law directly enacted by the UK Parliament. It may take two
forms: an Act of Parliament, *e.g.* Employment Rights Act 1996,
Employment Relations Act 1999; or a Statutory Instrument,
brought into effect by an individual Minister under the authority of an enabling Act, *e.g.* Working Time Regulations (SI
1998/1833), The Transfer of Undertakings (Protection of
Employment) Regulations 1981 (SI 1981/1794).

Both of these forms of legislation are, of course, directly
enforceable in the UK courts, and may be equally relied upon.

Case Law

Although over the past 30 years Employment Law has become
dominated by statute, case law is still very important. Not only
does case law both interpret the statute and fill in the gaps
between statutes, but certain areas of Employment Law are still
heavily dependent upon the common law, *e.g.* claims for wrongful dismissal.

An example of case law interpreting legislation would be:

The Race Relations Act 1976 refers to "ethnic origin", the case
of *Mandla v Dowell Lee* [1983] I.C.R. 385, HL laid down a test to
interpret this term and determine the conditions to be met by a
group wishing to bring itself within the protection of the Race
Relations Act. Consequently, if you were asked in an examination to consider whether discrimination in an employment
context against, *e.g.* an inhabitant of the Isle of Wight was
unlawful, you would need to consider first the statute itself and
then the subsequent case law in arriving at your answer.

European Law

It is outside the scope of this book to consider the detail of the legislative process of the EU, but there are several issues you will need to remember:

(a) EU law is supreme over national law. In any conflict between the two, European law will take precedence.

(b) Many Treaty Articles have been shown to be directly effective, both vertically (may be relied upon in a national court by an individual against the state) and horizontally (may be relied upon in a national court by an individual against another individual).

Of particular importance in Employment Law is Art.141, which states that men and women should receive equal pay for equal work. Article 141 was held to be directly effective by the European Court of Justice (ECJ) in the case of *Defrenne v Sabena* (Case 43/75).

(c) A Directive is an instruction to a Member State to adapt its law to conform to EU requirements.

A Directive may have direct effect if it is sufficiently clear and precise, but may only be relied upon by an individual in a national court against the state or an emanation of the state; in other words a Directive may have vertical direct effect only.

(d) The ECJ plays a very important part in the UK judicial system, in particular in the field of Employment Law. Questions on points of EU law may be referred to the ECJ under Art.234 by any national court. The decision or opinion of the ECJ will in practice be binding on the national court, both in the instant case and also as precedent for future cases, (although you should remember that the ECJ itself is not bound by its own previous decisions). Consequently, decisions of the ECJ referring to cases within other Member States of the EU will also form precedents for UK national courts.

2. THE TRIBUNAL AND COURT SYSTEM

Employment Tribunals (previously known as Industrial Tribunals) have jurisdiction to hear almost all individual disputes based on statutory employment law claims and, in addition, common law contract claims arising from or outstanding at the termination of employment up to a maximum of £25,000.

An Employment Tribunal is normally comprised of three members: a chairperson, being a barrister or solicitor of at least seven years' standing; and two lay members, drawn from either side of industry, one having had experience as perhaps a trade union official, the other having had management or trade association experience. Although it is uncommon, it is possible for the lay members to outvote the legally qualified chair.

The tribunal system was set up with the aims that it should be quicker, cheaper, more efficient and more accessible than the normal court system. In much of this it has been successful, although delays are not now uncommon partly due to the increased number of claims being made, and also partly due to the increased use of legal representation, particularly by employers, which tends to slow the system down.

There are a number of advantages and disadvantages to the tribunal system, and these include:

(a) Informality, lack of ceremony, regalia, etc. Hearings are normally conducted in a room, which although perhaps purpose built, is very similar to any meeting or small function room.

(b) Representation may be by the party themselves, a lawyer, a trade union representative, a friend, etc., although it should be noted that most companies tend to be legally represented.

(c) Legal Aid is not available for first instance tribunal hearings, but may be available for appeal hearings before the Employment Appeals Tribunal (EAT).

(d) Costs are rarely awarded; thus there is no financial threat to an applicant wishing to bring a claim.

(e) The members of the tribunal are specialist and experienced in employment disputes. Unlike magistrates or judges, members of an employment tribunal hear only cases within one area of law.

(f) Certain rules of evidence, *e.g.* hearsay, do not apply.

The procedure for bringing a complaint before an Employment Tribunal is fairly straightforward. The applicant completes a form and sends it to the tribunal office. A copy of the form is then sent to the employer who has 14 days in which to respond. Both the original form and the employer's response are then copied and sent to the Advisory Conciliation and Arbitration Service (ACAS), who may then attempt to obtain a settlement between the parties. If the claim is not settled at this stage, the tribunal will then make a preliminary examination of the case and may hold a pre-hearing review, often consisting of a tribunal chairperson sitting alone; this is in order to "weed out" particularly weak cases. Once a case goes to a full tribunal hearing the procedure adopted is similar in many ways to a court hearing; normally open to the public, it is basically an adversarial procedure, with each party putting its case, witnesses may be called and examined, other evidence introduced. However, unlike judges in most court hearings, the members of the tribunal take a much more active role in proceedings, questioning the parties and, if appropriate, leading applicants through the hearing procedure.

It is now standard practice for the tribunal to give the reasons for its decision in summary form, rather than in extended form, although this does not apply to cases of equal pay or discrimination.

If the applicant's claim is successful the tribunal may award any of three remedies: reinstatement, re-engagement or compensation. Perhaps not surprisingly, the most often awarded remedy is compensation—although when the tribunal system was first introduced it was thought that reinstatement or re-engagement would be the most commonly sought remedies.

An appeal against a decision of an Employment Tribunal on a point of law only may be made to the EAT. The EAT has the similar standing and many of the same powers as the High Court, and an appeal from the EAT goes to the Court of Appeal, and on occasion from there to the House of Lords.

The Employment Tribunal is bound by the decisions of the EAT and other superior courts; the EAT, whilst its own previous decisions are only persuasive, is bound by decisions of the Court of Appeal and the House of Lords.

3. WHO IS AN EMPLOYEE?

Employment Law governs the relationship between the employer and the employee.

Employers and employees have various rights, duties and liabilities to and for each other in law.

(a) An employer may have vicarious liability for the actions of his employees in the course of their employment.
(b) An employer has a duty to deduct income tax and National Insurance contributions from employees' wages.
(c) An employer owes a particular standard of care to his employees in regard to Health and Safety.
(d) An employer is bound by the terms and conditions of the contract of employment.
(e) Likewise, an employee is also bound by the contract of employment.
(f) An employee has the right not to be unfairly dismissed by his employer.
(g) In many circumstances an employee has the right to redundancy payments, the right to statutory notice periods, statutory holidays and statutory time off, etc.

It is therefore essential to be able to identify "an employee", and to differentiate between employees and self-employed workers, sometimes called "independent contractors", who are generally not covered by the same laws and rules.

DEFINITIONS AND TESTS

Statutory definition

Often it is not difficult to identify an employee. Section 230(1) of the Employment Rights Act 1996 (ERA) states, "In this Act 'employee' means an individual who has entered into or works under . . . a contract of employment." The Act goes on to state in s.230(2), "In this Act 'contract of employment' means a contract of service or apprenticeship, whether express or implied, and (if it is express) whether oral or in writing."

Problems do sometimes arise though in differentiating between employees and self-employed workers; whereas employees work under a contract of employment or a contract of service, a self-employed worker, or independent contractor, works under a contract for services.

It is not always easy to distinguish between the two, as for instance in the following brief examples:

(a) A sales representative who works exclusively for a company from their offices, but supplies his own car and is paid gross, without deduction of tax or National Insurance.
(b) An accounts clerk who has worked from home on a part-time basis for a company over a number of years.
(c) A part-time lecturer who regularly works for two or more universities during each academic year.

Over the years the courts have developed and applied various tests in an effort to formally determine who is an employee.

The Control Test

Formulated in the case of *Yewens v Noakes* (1880) 6 Q.B. 530 by Bramwell L.J., where he stated, "A servant is a person subject to the command of his master as to the manner in which he shall do his work." However, as working practices have changed over the years, and as industry has become more technical and required more specialist expertise, it has become obvious that the control test alone will not suffice. As Cooke J. stated in the case of *Market Investigations v Minister of Social Security* [1969] 2 Q.B. 173, ". . . control will no doubt always have to be considered, although it can no longer be regarded as the sole determining factor".

The Integration Test

Proposed and adopted by Denning L.J. from *Cassidy v Ministry of Health* [1951] 2 K.B. 353 and applied in *Stevenson Jordan & Harrison v MacDonald and Evans* [1952] T.L.R. 101, the integration test asked whether the worker's work is an integral part of the business, if so, the worker is an employee. If the worker's work is merely accessory to the business, then the worker is an independent contractor. The problem with the test is that it appears to call for a value judgment by the court without explaining the steps necessary in arriving at that judgment. Perhaps not surprisingly the test found little favour generally.

Multiple or Economic Reality Test

Proposed in the case of *Ready Mixed Concrete (South East) Ltd v Minister of Pensions & National Insurance* [1968] 2 Q.B. 497 by McKenna J., it asked three questions:

(a) Did the servant agree to provide his work in consideration of a wage or other remuneration?
(b) Did he agree, either expressly or impliedly, to be subject to the other's control to a sufficient degree to make the other master?
(c) Are the other provisions of the contract consistent with it being a contract of service?

McKenna J. also pointed out that "a man does not cease to run a business on his own account because he agrees to run it efficiently or to accept another's superintendence."

The Business Test

In many ways, this test is an extension of the Multiple or Economic Reality Test. It was formulated in the case of *Market Investigations v Minister of Social Security* [1969] 2 Q.B. 173 by Cooke J. and asks the fundamental question, Is the worker in business on their own account? It then considers such factors as control, whether the worker provides his own equipment, whether he hires his own helpers, what degree of financial risk he runs, whether the worker has responsibility for investment and management of the work and what, if any, opportunity the worker has to profit from the sound management of the task. In the later case of *Lee Ting Sang v Chung Chi-Keung* [1990] I.R.L.R. 236, the Privy Council stated that whilst there was no single test for determining employment status, the standard to be applied was best stated by the test from *Market Investigations*.

The Mutuality of Obligation Test

This test has been used on a number of occasions, particularly to try to determine the status of part-time, casual or "agency" workers.

It was used in the case of *O'Kelly v Trusthouse Forte plc* [1983] 3 All E.R. 456 to prove that part-time casual catering workers were not employees, since the court found that the company were under no obligation to provide work, and the workers were under no obligation to accept work if it were offered.

The importance of this factor was confirmed by the House of Lords in the case of *Carmichael v National Power Plc* [1999] I.C.R. 1226 which made clear that both control and mutuality of obligation are essential features of a contract of employment. Moreover, the test for mutuality of obligation must be applied in a contractual manner; in other words, the worker must be under a contractual obligation to accept work and the company under a contractual obligation to offer it. An attempt by the Court of Appeal in *Carmichael* [1998] I.R.L.R. 30 to mollify the test by introducing the element of reasonableness was firmly rejected by the House of Lords.

A rather different approach was adopted in the earlier case of *Nethermere (St Neots) Ltd v Taverna and Gardiner* [1984] I.R.L.R. 240, a case concerning the employment status of outworkers or home workers. A similar test was applied to show that although mutuality of obligation as such did not exist, the existence of "well founded expectations of continuing home work" could, over the period of a year or more, give rise to the existence of a contract of employment. Thus the home workers were employees.

Other Approaches

In recent years the courts have appeared to adopt a somewhat different approach. Rather than applying formalistic tests, there are several instances of the courts taking a more holistic approach. In the case of *Hall (HM Inspector of Taxes) v Lorimer* [1994] I.R.L.R. 171 concerning income tax assessment on either schedule D or schedule E basis, the court warned against the application of "mechanical tests", and took the view that each case should be decided on its own facts. In that case, the number of different companies the respondent had worked for and the short duration of each engagement were important factors—although they were not factors specifically considered in previous tests—in enabling the court to find that Mr Lorimer was self-employed.

In *Lane v Shire Roofing Co (Oxford) Ltd* [1995] I.R.L.R. 493, the facts of which showed similarities with several earlier cases, the Court of Appeal, whilst referring with approval to the line of authority and various tests defining employment status, were at pains to point out that the facts must be viewed and any tests applied with reference to modern working practices. In this case involving personal injury, Mr Lane was found to be an employee.

It would therefore seem that, on occasions, the courts have become more willing to hold that workers may be employees, even in those areas where traditionally it has been accepted that they were engaged on a self-employed basis.

OTHER ISSUES

On the topic of employee status, a number of other issues need to be considered.

Substitution

In both the *RMC Case* and the later case of *Express & Echo Publications Ltd v Tanton* [1999] I.R.L.R. 367 the courts have been influenced in their decisions by the power of the worker to provide a substitute, rather than undertake the work himself. In view of the personal nature of the employment contract, courts have accepted that if the worker has the authority to provide a substitute to do the work on their behalf, it is very unlikely that the worker's contract will be a contract of employment.

Self Description

Even if the parties themselves agree on the employment status of the worker, this may by no means be conclusive to the courts. In the case of *Ferguson v John Dawson & Ptns (Contractors) Ltd* [1976] 3 All E.R. 817, even when the worker gave a false name— presumably in order to avoid payment of tax—and both parties had agreed that he was employed on a self employed basis, the court by a majority decision still held that the company were his employer and that he was working under a contract of employment. As Browne L.J. stated: "The parties cannot by a label decide the true nature of their relationship".

Ferguson is often discussed in conjunction with the later case of *Massey v Crown Life Insurance Co* [1978] I.C.R. 590, in which a manager took professional advice and decided to change his employment status, with agreement from his employer, from employee to self-employed for tax reasons. Some two years later Mr Massey was dismissed and wished to claim for unfair dismissal—an option which was only open to him if he was held to be an employee. Based on the decision in *Ferguson*, it perhaps appeared that he had a strong case to succeed. However, the court held that he was self-employed, Lord Denning M.R. famously stating: "Having made his bed as being self-employed, he must lie on it."

The two decisions appear to conflict although the cases on their facts appear somewhat similar. They may however, perhaps be reconciled; *Ferguson* concerned a labourer who, in order to obtain work, joined a company on the basis on which they hired—a supposed independent-contractor status, the "lump" —he himself having little say in the matter. *Massey* concerned a senior employee who took professional advice and chose to change his status for his own financial advantage. The major difference between the cases, however, is the reason that they came before the courts; *Ferguson* concerning liability for personal injury, and *Massey* for a claim for unfair dismissal compensation. The courts often appear more willing to find employee status in favour of the applicant in cases concerning injury, than in those which involve tax or dismissal claims.

Fact or Law?

The Court of Appeal in the case of *O'Kelly v Trusthouse Forte Plc* [1983] 3 All E.R. 456 stated that it had for over 70 years been established law that the employment status of an individual was a question of fact, rather than a question of law. This was reiterated by the Privy Council in *Lee Ting Sang v Chung Chi-Keung* [1990] I.R.L.R. 236. The significance of this is that an appellate court should not interfere with a finding of fact, unless to use the words of Lord Simonds in *Edwards v Bairstow* [1956] A.C. 14 the trial court took "a view of the facts which could not reasonably be entertained". In other words, it is generally not possible to appeal against a finding of fact.

On occasion, however, the question of employment status may turn solely on the examination and interpretation of a document, as was the case in *The President of the Methodist Conference v Parfitt* [1984] I.R.L.R. 141. In such a case, the Court of Appeal ruled, the question would become a question of law, and an appellate court would thus have jurisdiction to interfere if necessary.

Agency Workers

The status of "agency workers" or "temps" is still in many cases unresolved.

The case of *Wickens v Champion Employment* [1984] I.C.R. 365 suggested that agency workers were not employees, since the:

> "relationship between the employers and temporaries seems to us wholly to lack the elements of continuity, and care of the employer for the employee, that one associates with a contract of service".

However, the Court of Appeal in *McMeechan v Secretary of State for Employment* [1997] I.R.L.R. 353 held that a temporary worker can have the status of employee of the employment agency in respect of each individual assignment worked, and this is supported by the Court of Appeal in the case of *Clark v Oxfordshire Health Authority* [1998] I.R.L.R. 125.

However, the recent case of *Montgomery v Johnson Underwood Ltd* [2001] I.C.R. 819 casts doubt on this reasoning. The Court of Appeal, following the House of Lords in *Carmichael*, pointed out that both control and mutuality of obligation must be present before a contract of employment can be identified. In the case of agency workers, although mutuality of obligation may exist between the agency and the worker, control over the worker is exercised on a day-to-day basis not by the agency but by the client company. Thus, it is argued, agency workers will apparently not be employees of either the agency or the client company. The court suggested that they may have a contract *sui generis*, since in most cases it is obvious that the worker is not a genuine self-employed independent contractor.

Commentary

It may therefore be seen that the apparently simple question of "Who is an employee?" has in fact presented the courts with problems over the years. One reason for this, and for the at times seemingly inconsistent decisions of the courts, may be the reasons that the question has been asked. In cases concerning vicarious liability or personal injury, *e.g. Lane v Shire Roofing Co (Oxford) Ltd* [1995] I.R.L.R. 493, it seems that the courts have been very willing to find employee status despite often strong evidence to the contrary. Indeed in the *Lane* case it may be argued that the application of almost any of the traditional tests would have produced a contrary result.

Other Legislation

Certain Employment Law statutes are designed to have a wider effect than others by including more than only "employees".

Equal Pay Act 1970 (EqPA) has a wider definition of "employed" and s.1(6)(a) of the EqPA 1970 states "'employed' means employed under a contract of service or of apprenticeship or a contract personally to execute any work or labour."

Sex Discrimination Act 1975 (SDA) applies in an employment context to applicants for work, employees and contract workers. Again the wider definition of "employed" is used in the SDA (s.82 of the SDA 1975).

Race Relations Act 1976 (RRA) follows the SDA very closely in format. The wider definition of "employed" is again used (s.78 of the RRA 1976).

Disability Discrimination Act 1995 (DDA) defines "employment" again as "employment under a contract of service or of apprenticeship or a contract personally to do any work" (s.68(1) of the DDA 1995).

Employment Relations Act 1999 (ERelA) grants to the Secretary of State the power to extend a range of employment rights to various categories of workers who may not technically qualify as employees, *e.g.* agency workers.

---

4. THE CONTRACT OF EMPLOYMENT

In many respects the contract of employment is very similar to any other contract. Usually, a contract of employment will be expressed in writing, but as with many other contracts this need not always be the case. A statutory definition is given as "a contract of service or apprenticeship, whether express or implied, and (if it is express) whether oral or in writing" (s.230(2)of the ERA 1996).

The contract of employment will consist of a number of terms and conditions. These may be either express terms or implied terms. Express terms are those terms which have been agreed between the parties, either orally or in writing. Implied terms are those which are so obvious to an onlooker that they are held to be part of the contract, and therefore do not need to be expressed by the parties. Many text books will include among the implied terms those imposed by statute.

Breach by either party of any of the terms of the contract will, of course, amount to a breach of contract; if the term is held to be a fundamental term of the contract, the breach would allow the injured party to treat the contract as terminated, and act accordingly.

EXPRESS TERMS

Under s.1 of the ERA 1996 every employer must give to each employee, within two months of the commencement of employment, a written statement of the particulars of employment. Failure to provide the statement within two months allows the employee to complain to an employment tribunal under s.11 of the ERA 1996, and the tribunal may decide what particulars should be included.

This "section 1 statement" must include:

(a) the names of the employer and employee;

(b) the date on which the employment began.

(c) the date on which the employee's period of continuous employment began, which would take into account any previous employment which counts as continuous;

(d) the scale and/or rate of remuneration;

(e) intervals at which remuneration is paid;

(f) terms and conditions regarding hours of work;

(g) details regarding holidays and holiday pay;

(h) details regarding sickness/injury and sick pay (here the employee may be referred to a separate document);

(i) pension and pension scheme provisions (here the employee may be referred to a separate document);

(j) notice periods;

(k) in the case of temporary positions, the length of contract or expected date of termination;

(l) place(s) of work;

(m) any collective agreements which may affect the terms and conditions of employment (these details may be provided in a separate document);

(n) a note concerning disciplinary rules and procedures (here the employee may be referred to a separate document)—

this is not necessary where the total number of employees is less than 20; and

(o) some further details must be given if the employee is to work outside the UK.

It is common practice for employers to include all of these details in a written contract of employment, which, once signed by the parties becomes legally binding. If the employer does not choose to do this, a separate s.1 statement must then be issued; such a statement would not in itself be a contract (unless signed as a contract by the parties (*Gascol Conversions Ltd v Mercer* [1974] I.C.R. 420)) but would allow a tribunal to draw strong *prima facie* evidence of the contents of the employment contract (*System Floors (UK) Ltd v Daniel* [1982] I.C.R. 54).

Collective Bargaining

The results or products of collective bargaining may affect an individual's contract of employment by, in theory, any of three ways. The first and most obvious is by express incorporation into the contract. If a term is agreed upon by the parties whereby, for example, the rate of pay is affected by the collective agreement in force between the trade union and the employer, the rate of pay to the employee may be varied accordingly without the need for any further agreement (*Robertson v British Gas* [1983] I.R.L.R. 302). Such a term may be included in the contracts of employment of both union members and non-union members.

The second theory of incorporation into an individual employee's contract is by way of agency—the idea that the trade union is acting as agent for its members as individuals. Although the laws of agency may permit this, in practice it is most unlikely that either the union or its members would wish to be so bound. The case of *Burton Group v Smith* [1977] I.R.L.R. 351 is authority for the presumption that the trade union does not act as agent for its individual members in collective agreements.

Thirdly and finally it may be possible to incorporate the products of collective agreements (or indeed many other terms) into an individual's contract by conduct; in effect as part of custom and practice (see below).

It is, of course, possible for almost any term to become an express term of the contract, if agreed to by both parties; it appears that the Unfair Contract Terms Act 1977 applies to the contract of employment (*Johnstone v Bloomsbury Health Authority* [1992] Q.B. 333, *Brigden v American Express Bank* [2000] I.R.L.R. 94)—the contract is taken to operate with the employee as the consumer. It should, however, be noted that the wording of the Unfair Terms in Consumer Contracts Regulations 1994 specifically excludes employment contracts.

IMPLIED TERMS

On the Part of the Employer

It is generally held that an employer must comply with four major implied terms: a duty to pay wages; a duty to exercise reasonable care; a duty to provide a grievance procedure; and a duty of mutual trust and confidence.

Duty to pay wages. Wages are the major consideration for the work done by the employee. Unless expressly agreed, wages may not be paid in kind, but must be paid as money. However, there is no implied right for an employee to be paid in cash; payment may be made by credit transfer to the employee's bank, by cheque or by wage packet, etc.

Part II of the ERA 1996 protects employees from unauthorised deductions from wages. It does not, however, apply in the following situations:

(a) where the deduction is made under a statutory provision (s.13(1)(a) of the ERA 1996);

(b) where the deduction is made under a provision in the worker's contract of employment (s.13(1)(a) of the ERA 1996);

(c) where the worker has consented in writing to the deduction (s.13(1)(b) of the ERA 1996);

(d) where the deduction is the reimbursement for an overpayment in wages (s.14(1)(a) of the ERA 1996), although the deduction will normally only be permitted by the courts if the original overpayment was a mistake of fact (rather than a mistake of law), and even so the employer may be estopped from making the deduction if the employee had been led to believe the money to be his, had acted on that belief, and the overpayment had not been the fault of the employee (*Avon County Council v Howlett* [1983] I.R.L.R. 171);

(e) an overpayment of work related expenses (s.14(1)(b) of the ERA 1996) subject to similar conditions as (d) above; and

(f) where the deduction is made on account of the worker having taken part in a strike or other industrial action (s.14(5) of the ERA 1996). For application of this see the cases of *Miles v Wakefield Metropolitan District Council* [1987] I.R.L.R. 193 and *Wiluszynski v Tower Hamlets LBC* [1989] I.C.R. 493.

A failure to pay wages is held to constitute a deduction for the purpose of the ERA (*Delaney v Staples t/a De Montfort Recruitment* [1992] 1 A.C. 687), but a failure to pay monies in lieu of notice is not. Money in lieu of notice is traditionally held to be damages for wrongful dismissal, and not wages (*Delaney v Staples*). Be aware, however, of the decision in *EMI v Coldicott* [1999] I.R.L.R. 630, where it was held that if the payment of money in lieu of notice is made under authorisation of an express term of the employment contract, the money will be taken to be remuneration arising from the contract rather than being damages for breach of contract—as such, of course, the money will be liable to taxation.

If the issue of sick pay is not covered by an express term of the contract, the courts have held that there is no presumption of a right to wages when off sick; each case will be considered on its merits (*Mears v Safecar Security Ltd* [1960] Q.B. 54).

Generally there is no obligation on the part of the employer to provide work, as long as wages are paid (*Collier v Sunday Referee Publishing Co. Ltd* [1940] 2 K.B. 647), but the courts have identified two main areas where the employer may be under a duty to provide work:

(a) where payment is made on a commission or piecework basis (*Devonald v Rosser & Sons Ltd* [1906] 2 K.B. 728); and

(b) where an employee is engaged on skilled work and needs to continue to work to maintain or develop that level of skill (*Breach v Epsylon Industries Ltd* [1976] I.C.R. 316), or where publicity or public exposure is understood to form part of the consideration due to the employee, *e.g.* an entertainer, actor, etc. (*Turner v Sawdon & Co.* [1901] 2 K.B. 653).

Additionally, if the contract provides, either expressly or impliedly, that the work will be provided, failure by the employer to do so would amount to an actionable breach (*William Hill Organisation Ltd v Tucker* [1998] I.R.L.R. 313).

Duty to exercise reasonable care. At common law, the employer is under a duty to take reasonable care for the health and safety of his employees. The standard of care is "the care which an ordinary prudent employer would take in all the circumstances" (*Paris v Stepney Borough Council* [1951] 1 All E.R. 42). This duty is owed to employees as individuals (*Paris v Stepney Borough Council*), and consequently a higher standard of duty may be owed to some employees than to others (*James v Hepworth & Grandage Ltd* [1968] 1 Q.B. 94). The employer should provide safe plant and premises, a safe system of work and reasonably competent fellow employees.

Duty to provide a grievance procedure. The employer has a duty to both provide and effectively operate a grievance procedure (*WA Goold (Pearmak) Ltd v McConnell* [1995] I.R.L.R. 516). In the case of *Bracebridge Engineering Ltd v Darby* [1990] I.R.L.R. 3 it was held that failure to investigate or take seriously a complaint of sexual harassment constituted a fundamental breach of contract.

Duty of mutual trust and confidence. Sometimes also referred to as a duty to co-operate, or the duty of mutual co-operation. The duty has been defined by the court as an obligation on the employer that he should not "without reasonable and proper cause, conduct [himself] in a manner calculated to or likely to destroy or seriously damage the relationship of confidence and trust between employer and employee" (*Woods v WM Car Services (Peterborough) Ltd* [1981] I.C.R. 666.

Cases to illustrate a breach of this duty include:

(a) *Isle of Wight Tourist Board v Coombes* [1976] I.R.L.R. 413, where a manager said of his secretary that she was an "intolerable bitch on a Monday morning".
(b) *Post Office v Roberts* [1980] I.R.L.R. 347, where a senior manager wrote an unfavourable report on an employee without consideration of her work record, which resulted in her being refused promotion.

(c) *Malik v BCCI* [1997] I.R.L.R. 462, where the dishonest conduct of the employer may amount to a breach of mutual trust and confidence.

It should, of course, be remembered that conduct that may be acceptable in one particular industry or situation, may not be acceptable in another, and in those circumstances may be held to amount to a breach of the duty of trust and confidence. In recent years the courts have both widened the scope and increased the importance of the implied term of mutual trust and confidence (see, *e.g.* "Constructive Dismissal"). The recent case of *University of Nottingham v Eyett* [1998] I.R.L.R. 646 suggests that, although in previous cases the duty of trust and confidence has been expressed in a negative form, *i.e.* refraining from conduct likely to harm the relationship, in principle the duty may have a positive form, and in appropriate cases may be breached by a failure on the part of the employer to warn or act.

ON THE PART OF THE EMPLOYEE

The employee is also bound by a number of implied terms; these are generally held to be a duty of obedience, a duty to adapt, a duty to exercise care and a duty of fidelity or good faith.

Duty of obedience

An employee has a duty to obey all reasonable and lawful orders. The employer may not, however, order the employee to do an illegal act (*Morrish v Henlys (Folkestone) Ltd* [1973] I.C.R. 482), nor may the employer order the employee into immediate danger (*Ottoman Bank v Chakarian* [1930] A.C. 277).

Duty to adapt

Generally an employee has a duty to adapt to new methods and techniques introduced by the employer, in such cases though, the employer should provide appropriate training or retraining (*Cresswell v Board of Inland Revenue* [1984] I.C.R. 508).

In each case the court must decide whether the changes amount to merely an adaptation of the way in which the job is carried out, or a change of the job itself, in which case the question of redundancy may arise (*North Riding Garages Ltd v Butterwick* [1967] 2 Q.B. 56).

Duty to exercise care

The employee has a general duty to exercise reasonable care in the performance of his work.

The practical importance of this usually arises in an action in tort where the employee has acted negligently causing injury to a third party, and the employer is held vicariously liable for the employee's actions. In such a situation the employer may be able to sue the employee for an indemnity, either for breach of contract (*Lister v Romford Ice and Cold Storage Co Ltd* [1957] A.C. 555), or in tort, where both are held to be joint tortfeasors, for either a contribution or a full indemnity. It should be noted that both such actions are extremely rare, and in effect, are contrary to the notion of employer's vicarious liability.

Duty of fidelity or good faith

The courts have held that virtually any act by an employee which is inconsistent with the contract of employment and which does or may cause injury to the employer will amount to a breach by the employee of the duty of fidelity or good faith.

This duty may be broken down into several sub-headings:

(a) Duty to account for secret profits made by the employee in the course of his employment (*Boston Deep Sea Fishing and Ice Co v Ansell*).

(b) Duty not to compete with the employer whilst in employment (*Hivac Ltd v Park Royal Scientific Instruments Ltd* [1946] Ch. 169), although the courts are reluctant to place any unnecessary restrictions on an individual's spare time.

(c) Duty regarding competition by ex-employees. With the exception of an express contract term restraining an employee from competition after leaving the employment and a general protection of trade secrets (see "Restraint of Trade"), it may be difficult to show a duty of fidelity regarding an employee's actions following the termination of the contract of employment (although see the Australian case of *Ansell Rubber Co v Allied Rubber Industries* [1967] V.R. 37). Many actions which would constitute a breach of the duty of fidelity if carried out by an employee, may be quite lawful if carried out by an ex-employee.

Thus, most breaches of this duty are actually committed by employees prior to leaving their employment either to join another company or to set up business on their own. Examples of this include:

- *Wessex Dairies Ltd v Smith* [1935] 2 K.B. 80, canvassing his employer's customers prior to setting up his own business.
- *Robb v Green* [1895] 2 Q.B. 315, making or memorising a list of the employer's customers prior to setting up his own business.

(d) Duty to co-operate. In the cases of both *Secretary of State for Employment v ASLEF (No 2)* [1972] 2 Q.B. 455 and *Ticehurst v British Telecommunications Plc* [1992] I.R.L.R. 219 the courts have held that actions taken by employees with the intention of disrupting the employer's business may amount to a breach of contract; even though that action may be no more than a "work to rule", which by its very nature means working to the terms of the contract but no further.

Work Rules

Although the contract of employment will contain either an express or an implied term that the employee will abide by "the rules", unless individually specified in the contract, these rules may not have contractual force in themselves (*Secretary of State for Employment v ASLEF (No 2)* [1972] 2 Q.B. 455).

One effect of this is very much in favour of the employer, in that, although breach of the rules by the employee may be a breach of the contract term of duty to obey orders, since the rules themselves do not have contractual force, the employer may change them unilaterally without breaching the contract.

Custom and Practice

In reality, there is very little significance or importance today in the incorporation of terms into the contract of employment through custom and practice. For a term to be incorporated through custom and practice it should be notorious, certain and reasonable. The leading case is *Sagar v H Ridehalgh & Son Ltd* [1931] 1 Ch. 310.

Statute

The growth of statute as a source of employment law over the past few years has had considerable impact on the contract of employment. There are perhaps three ways in which statute may affect the actual contract terms:

(a) On occasion, statute directly imposes a term into the contract of employment, *e.g.* s.1(1) of the EqPA 1970 imposes an equality clause into the contracts of women, and by virtue of s.1(13) of the EqPA 1970 into the contracts of men.
(b) Statute may often operate to restrict or negate a contract term, *e.g.* both the SDA 1975 and Treaty Art.119 would make void any contract term which purported to restrict promotion prospects for women.
(c) Whilst breach by the employer of statute will normally be actionable by the employee in its own right, it may also amount to a breach of the duty of mutual trust and confidence.

CASE EXAMPLE

United Bank Ltd v Akhtar [1989] I.R.L.R. 507
A junior bank employee, whose contract contained an express mobility clause, was instructed to move from Leeds to the Birmingham offices of his employers, at only six days notice and with no financial assistance. He refused, partly due to family circumstances, left, and claimed unfair dismissal owing to his having been constructively dismissed.

Held: Despite the express mobility clause in the employment contract, the employee had been constructively dismissed, since, the EAT held, it was necessary to imply into the contract a requirement that the employer should not exercise a term in such a way that the employee was unable to comply with it.

Commentary: This decision, although undoubtedly fair on the facts, comes dangerously close to reintroducing the "reasonableness test", specifically rejected by the Court of Appeal in *Western Excavating*. A better way of looking at the decision would perhaps be to confirm that the employer was not in breach of contract by enforcing a contractual term, but that the way in which a term was invoked could breach the implied term of mutual trust and confidence. The breach of this implied term may then give grounds for constructive dismissal.

CASE EXAMPLE

Dryden v Greater Glasgow Health Board [1992] I.R.L.R. 469

Ms Dryden was employed as a nursing auxiliary in a Glasgow hospital. She smoked approximately 30 cigarettes per day. Due to the nature of her job, she was unable to leave the premises during the working day, but until 1991 areas had been set aside inside the hospital where smoking was permitted.

In 1991, following consultation, a policy was implemented banning smoking in all general and maternity hospitals. All staff were given notice of the change, and offered advice and counselling. 10 days after the policy was implemented Ms Dryden resigned and claimed she had been constructively dismissed.

Held: Dismissing her claim, the EAT stated that there was no implied term that an employee was permitted to smoke at work, nor had the employers acted in such a way so as to prevent the employee from carrying out her part of the contract, therefore they had not breached the duty of mutual trust and confidence.

An employer is entitled to make rules for the conduct of their employees, and if a rule is introduced for a legitimate purpose, the fact that it bears hard on a particular employee does not in itself lead to a breach of contract.

Commentary: Two issues may be considered. First, Ms Dryden had worked at the hospital for some 14 years, during all of which time she had smoked with the implied permission of her employer. It was not, however, fully argued whether a "right to smoke" may have been implied into her employment contract through either conduct or custom and practice. Secondly, although, because of the generally accepted health risks through even passive smoking, the majority would probably not oppose a no-smoking rule in a hospital, how likely is it that a similar decision would have been reached in different but comparable circumstances?

---

5. EQUAL PAY

The law regarding equal pay is in principle very basic and straightforward. It states simply that men and women should receive equal pay regardless of gender.

However, aspects of the legislation and much of the case law have succeeded in complicating and at times confusing this otherwise simple doctrine.

Equal pay legislation in the UK is twofold: national legislation—the EqPA 1970 as amended; and Art.141 of the Treaty of Rome, along with the explanatory EU Directives nos. 75/117 and 76/207.

In the case of *Pickstone v Freemans Plc* [1988] I.R.L.R. 357, the House of Lords stated that the EqPA must be interpreted purposively in line with Art.141 and Directive 75/117. Normally, therefore, a national court will have no need nor authority to consider Art.141 if the EqPA provides a full and adequate remedy (*Blaik v Post Office* [1994] I.R.L.R. 280).

The Equal Pay Act 1970 (as amended)

It is possible for a woman or a man to bring a claim for equal pay under any of three heads within the EqPA. In each case it is necessary that the applicant select a comparator, who must be of the opposite sex. The choice of comparator is for the applicant to make (*Picksone v Freemans Plc*), but may not be a hypothetical comparator although it may be a predecessor (*Macarthys Ltd v Smith* [1980] I.C.R. 672). The applicant may choose either a single comparator or multiple comparators (*Hayward v Cammell Laird Shipbuilders* [1988] I.C.R. 464). If the applicant is unable to name a comparator, they may be granted discovery to enable them to obtain sufficient details—however such discovery may not be used as a "fishing trip" permitting an applicant to trawl through personnel records in search of likely comparators, etc. (*Leverton v Clwyd County Council* [1989] I.C.R. 33). It is also necessary that both the applicant and the comparator(s) are employed either by the same employer at the same establishment, or by the same or associated employer at an establishment at which "common terms and conditions of employment are observed" (*Leverton v Clwyd County Council*). The House of Lords in *British Coal Corp v Smith* [1996] I.R.L.R. 404 took a broad approach to this, stating that it was sufficient that the terms should be "substantially comparable". On the issue of choice of comparators, it is worth considering the recent case of *South Ayrshire Council v Morton* [2002] I.R.L.R. 256, which may extend the range available to certain applicants.

The three heads of claim are: like work, work rated as equivalent and work of equal value.

Like work. Section 1 EqPA 1970 states that an applicant may bring a claim if the work they do is "the same" as or of "a broadly similar nature" to the work done by their chosen comparator; and the work will be of a broadly similar nature if any differences are of no practical importance. In the case of *Capper Pass Ltd v Lawton* [1977] I.C.R. 83, the EAT adopted a "broad brush approach" in holding that the work done by the applicant, the directors' cook, was sufficiently similar to the work done by cooks in the works canteen for the claim to succeed.

Likewise, in the case of *Shields v E Coombes (Holdings) Ltd* [1978] I.C.R. 1159 where male counterhands were paid more than their female counterparts since, according to the employer, the men acted not only "as a deterrent to attack . . . or other trouble" but also to deal with any such trouble until the police arrived, the Court of Appeal held that since in the previous three years there had been no such trouble, the additional responsibilities of the men were of no practical importance. Consequently, the applicant's claim succeeded.

However, in cases where differences relate to genuine differences in levels of responsibility or consequences of mistakes, these differences may be sufficient to defeat a claim (*Eaton Ltd v Nuttall* [1977] I.C.R. 272).

A three stage approach was set out by Bridge L.J. in *Shields v Coombes* for claims based on like work:

> "First, was their work of the same or a broadly similar nature? Second, if so, were any differences between the things she did and the things he did (regard being had to the frequency, nature and extent of such differences) of practical importance . . . Third . . . Can the employer then prove that any variation between the woman's contract and the man's is genuinely due to a material difference (other than the difference of sex) between her case and his?"

Work rated as equivalent. If a job evaluation scheme has been carried out and agreed by the parties (*Arnold v Beecham Group* [1982] I.R.L.R. 307) it may be relied upon to found a claim for equal pay. The job evaluation study must, of course, be objective (*Rummler v Dato-Druck GmbH* [1987] I.C.R. 774).

Work of equal value. Following the case of *EC Commission v United Kingdom* (Case 165/82), legislation was introduced to bring the EqPA into line with Art.141 and Directive 75/117. This resulted in the Equal Pay (Amendment) Regulations 1983 bringing into effect the third head of claim—work of equal value. Section 1(1)(c) of the EqPA 1970 states:

> "where a woman is employed on work which . . . is, in terms of the demands made on her (for instance under such headings as effort, skill and decision), of equal value to that of a man in the same employment. . ."

It is for the applicant to choose under which head they wish to bring their claim, although they must consider whether a claim under "like work" would be more appropriate; they may wish to claim under "equal value" even if *prima facie* there is an available comparator to enable a claim under "like work" (*Pickstone v Freemans Plc*). This prevents the employer from employing a token male on like work and so avoiding the purpose of the legislation.

The procedure involved in an equal value claim is as follows. Once the claim has been brought to the tribunal, the tribunal must consider whether there are, *prima facie*, reasonable grounds for determining that the work is of equal value. If so, the tribunal may commission an independent expert to carry out a study of the work in question and report to the tribunal. The tribunal would then adjourn, probably for several months, while the expert report is prepared. Although it is usual for the tribunal to accept the expert's report in full, it does not have to. There are occasions where a part of the report has been ignored (*Wells v F Smales & Sons Ltd* (1985) 281 I.R.L.I.B. 11), or where the report's conclusion has been rejected entirely (*Tennants Textile Colours Ltd v Todd* [1989] I.R.L.R. 3). The employer can, at the initial stage, prevent the appointment of an expert by successfully introducing a defence of genuine material factor, which if successful will defeat the claim.

Genuine material factor defence

A claim for equal pay may be defeated "if the employer proves that the variation [in pay] is genuinely due to a material factor which is not the difference of sex. . ." (s.1(3) of the EqPA 1970).

The Act goes on to state that in the case of claims for "like work" or "work rated as equivalent" the material factor *must* be a material difference, whereas in a claim for "equal value" the material factor *may* be such a material difference. This would seem to suggest that wider defences are open for claims of "equal value". However case law does not support this contention, and it is probably safe to assume that defences for all three heads of claim are to be treated in the same way.

Those material factors which refer specifically to the individual worker will not normally present any problems to the tribunal. It is quite acceptable that factors such as length of service, seniority, responsibility or qualifications may be acceptable as defences.

However, problems may arise with factors which are due to the operation of the employer's business or more general market factors. It is worth considering some of these in some detail:

(a) Red-circling, where an internal reorganisation reduces the grade of some workers but allows them to retain their previous salary scale. If the red-circling is discriminatory or has been brought about by some past discrimination it will not be permitted as a valid defence (*Snoxell v Vauxhall Motors Ltd* [1977] I.C.R. 700). In any event, red-circling should not exist any longer than is necessary.

(b) Collective agreements may be accepted as defences, but they must be genuinely operated, transparent in classification systems and not tainted by any discriminatory attitudes. It is for the employer to rebut any suggestions of discrimination and explain how any job evaluation study worked (see, *Rummler v Dato-Druck GmbH* Case 237/85 [1986] E.C.R. 2101, *Danfoss* Case 109/88 [1989] I.R.L.R. 532).

(c) Performance related pay, commission based, piecework or target related. It is for the employer to show objective justification for any pay differences between men and women, in much the same way as for collective agreements (*Royal Copenhagen* Case C–400/93 [1995] I.R.L.R. 648).

(d) Part-time working. Traditionally most part-time workers have been women, thus discrimination against part-timers is indirect discrimination against women, and will be *prima facie* unlawful. However, discrimination in fringe pay, *e.g.* overtime and shift allowances may be permissable if it can be objectively justified (*Calder v Rowntree Mackintosh Confectionary Ltd* [1993] I.R.L.R. 212).

(e) Market forces. At first glance, it would appear that a "market forces" defence should succeed. If a company is able to attract a class or group of people to work for less than others it would make sound financial sense to do so. However, considering the inequalities of bargaining power in employment and the fact that traditionally men have been able to command higher wages than women, to allow such a *carte blanche* defence would obviously seriously undermine both domestic and EU legislation.

The approach of the courts is demonstrated in the following cases:

(a) *Rainey v Greater Glasgow Health Board* [1987] I.C.R. 129, the House of Lords held that market forces may constitute a defence if they amounted to a genuine, objective reason. Although this decision has been criticised, it may be justified if viewed as a form of red-circling, particularly if viewed in the light of the following case.

(b) *Benveniste v University of Southampton* [1989] I.R.L.R. 122, where the court held that market forces could only amount to a genuine material factor defence for as long as those particular facts existed. Once the market or financial constraints eased, the defence would no longer be available.

(c) *Enderby v Frenchay HA* [1994] I.C.R. 112, in which the ECJ stated that it was "for the national court to determine, if necessary by applying the principle of proportionality, whether and to what extent the shortage of candidates for a job and the need to attract them by higher pay constitutes an objectively justified economic ground for the difference in pay. . ."

(d) *Ratcliffe v North Yorkshire CC* [1995] I.R.L.R. 439 where the House of Lords held that the employer could not cut the wages of employees in order to compete with an external contractor for a competitive tender, thus denying a market forces defence.

CASE EXAMPLE

Glasgow City Council v Marshall **[2000] I.R.L.R. 272**
There were eight applicants in the case, seven female and one male. All were instructors in special schools in Scotland and claimed equal pay with teachers working in the same schools. The female instructors named a male teacher as comparator and the male instructor named a female teacher. It was accepted that although teachers had higher qualifications than the instructors, both groups performed the same or broadly similar work. It was therefore for the employers to establish a s.1(3) defence, which they did by arguing both that the pay structure was the result of collective negotiations, and also by introducing statistical evidence to show that the pay structures did not discriminate on the grounds of gender.

Held: The claim would fail since all instructors, both male and female, were paid the same "instructor" rate as agreed by collective bargaining, and all teachers, whether male or female were paid at the same agreed "teacher" rate—thus, differences in pay were not the result of discrimination on the grounds of sex.
The House of Lords laid down a four stage approach:

(a) the explanation for differences in pay must be genuine,
(b) as a question of causation, the less favourable treatment complained of is due to that reason,
(c) the reason is not the difference of sex, either directly or indirectly, and
(d) that the factor relied upon is a material difference between the woman's case and the man's case.

Commentary: As Lord Slynn stated: "This is plainly in essence a claim that the pay is not fair; and not a claim that the pay is unequal because of discrimination between the sexes. As such, it does not fall within the Equal Pay Act 1970."

What is Pay?

Section 1 of the EqPA 1970 states, in relation to like work, work rated as equivalent and work of equal value:

"(i) If . . . any term of the woman's contract is or becomes less favourable to the woman than a term of a similar kind in the contract under which that man is employed, that term of the woman's contract shall be treated as so modified as not to be less favourable, and

(ii) If . . . at any time the woman's contract does not include a term corresponding to a term benefiting that man included in the contract under which he is employed, the woman's contract shall be treated as including such a term."

Consequently, the courts have held the following:

(a) Each term in the contract should be equalised, not just the overall package—despite initial fears of "leap-frogging" (*Hayward v Cammell Laird Shipbuilders*).
(b) Occupational pensions are pay (*Barber v Guardian Royal Exchange* [1990] I.C.R. 616).
(c) Sick pay is pay (*Rinner-Kuhn v FWW Spezial-Gebaudereinigung GmbH* [1989] I.R.L.R. 493).
(d) Pay for attending training courses is pay (*Arbeiterwohlfahrt der Stadt Berlin eV v Botel* [1992] I.R.L.R. 423).
(e) Rules governing pay increments are pay (*Nimz v Freie und Hansestadt Hamburg* [1991] I.R.L.R. 222).
(f) *Ex gratia* termination payments are pay (*Barber v Guardian Royal Exchange*).
(g) Redundancy payments are pay (*Barber v Guardian Royal Exchange*).
(h) Compensation for unfair dismissal is pay (*R. v Secretary of State, Ex p. Seymour-Smith and Perez* [1999] E.C.J.).

However, social security payments, including, *e.g.* unemployment benefit, state pensions, etc., would fall outside the ambit of Art.141 or the EqPA.

Although the EPA 1970 set a two-year limitation period for claiming arrears of pay, following the ECJ case of *Levez v TH Jennings (Harlow Pools) Ltd* [1999] I.R.L.R. 26, a six-year limitation period is now applied.

CASE EXAMPLE

Hayward v Cammell Laird Shipbuilders **[1988] I.C.R. 464**
Ms Hayward, who was employed as a cook, brought a claim for equal pay, by claiming that her work was of equal value with

that of male painters, joiners and insulation fitters employed by the same company.

Held: Her claim succeeded. Furthermore, it was held that the individual components of the pay packages of Ms Hayward and her comparators should be equalised, not just the overall total.

Commentary: This is a useful case, since it is good authority for several propositions: an applicant may choose their own comparator; an applicant may choose multiple comparators if they wish; individual components of pay should be compared and equalised, not just the overall package; the supposed danger of "leap-frogging" does not constitute a defence; and finally, it is the first case of an equal value claim brought in this country.

6. DISCRIMINATION

At a basic level, "discrimination" means nothing more than choice. However, in an employment context the word has taken on a rather different meaning, and is used in a somewhat negative sense.

In employment, it is unlawful to discriminate against an employee or potential employee on the grounds of sex, race or disability.

Some legislative protection is given to those with criminal records, under the Rehabilitation of Offenders Act 1974, and in Northern Ireland it is unlawful to discriminate on the grounds of religion or political opinion (Fair Employment (Northern Ireland) Act 1989). Legislation is planned throughout the UK in 2003 making it unlawful to discriminate on the grounds of religion or belief; furthermore, it is expected that legislation regarding age discrimination will come into effect in 2006.

Since the Race Relations Act 1976 follows the Sex Discrimination Act 1975 very closely, and much of the case law is interchangeable, it is convenient to examine both sex and race discrimination together, and to look at disability discrimination separately.

SEX AND RACE DISCRIMINATION

Scope of the existing legislation

Both the Sex Discrimination Act 1975 (SDA) and the Race
Relations Act 1976 (RRA) cover all aspects of employment, from
the recruitment process, through the working relationship, to
the termination.

Both the SDA and the RRA apply not only to those working
under a contract of service, *i.e.* "employees", but also to those
under a contract to personally execute any work or labour, *i.e.*
"self-employed independent contractors" (s.82 of the SDA 1975
and s.78 of the RRA 1976).

There is no minimum qualifying period necessary in order to
gain protection under the legislation, indeed, as stated above,
the Acts will apply even before the employment relationship is
confirmed.

**Equal Opportunities Commission (EOC), the Commission for
Racial Equality (CRE) and the Disability Rights Commission
(DRC)**

The EOC was set up under the SDA, and the CRE under the
RRA. Both have powers under the relevant Act to conduct
formal investigations, to issue non-discrimination notices, to act
in the case of discriminatory advertisements, to seek injunction
through the civil courts to restrain persistent offenders, and to
assist individuals in bringing actions. In 1999, the DRC was
formed under the DDA to perform a similar function to the EOC
and CRE. All three commissions are charged with reviewing
and recommending on policy and legislative issues.

The Sex Discrimination Act 1975

Although the SDA is phrased so as to apply to discrimination
against women, it applies equally to discrimination against men
(s.2(1) of the SDA 1975), with the exception of special treatment
afforded to women in connection with pregnancy and childbirth
(s.2(2) of the SDA 1975).

The SDA covers not only discrimination on the grounds of
gender, but also discrimination against married persons (s.3 of
the SDA 1975), although it does not cover discrimination against
unmarried persons.

The Race Relations Act 1976

The RRA covers discrimination on racial grounds. "Racial grounds" are defined as "colour, race, nationality or ethnic or national origins" (s.3(1) of the RRA 1976).

There is much case law to define more precisely the term "ethnic origin". The House of Lords in the case of *Mandla v Dowell Lee* [1983] I.R.L.R. 209 laid down a number of conditions to be considered for any group wishing to bring themselves within the protection of the Act:

(a) a long shared history, of which the group is conscious as distinguishing itself from other groups, and the memory of which it keeps alive; and

(b) a cultural tradition of its own, including family and social customs and manners, often but not necessarily associated with religious observance.

   Both of these the House of Lords held to be essential.

(c) a common geographical origin or descent from a small number of common ancestors;

(d) a common language, that need not be exclusive to the group;

(e) a common literature;

(f) a common religion, different from neighbouring or surrounding groups; and

(g) being a minority or oppressed or dominant group within a community.

These five conditions were held by the House of Lords to be important factors, but not essential.

Applying this "test" it was held in *Mandla v Dowell Lee* that Sikhs are an ethnic group.

Subsequent case law has decided the following:

(a) Jews are an ethnic group (*Seide v Gillette Industries* [1980] I.R.L.R. 427).

(b) Gypsies are an ethnic group (*CRE v Dutton* [1989] I.R.L.R. 8).

(c) Rastafarians are not an ethnic group (*Dawkins v Dept of the Environment* [1993] I.R.L.R. 284).

(d) Jehovah's Witnesses are not an ethnic or racial group (*Lovell-Badge v Norwich City College* Case 1502237/97).

(e) RRA covers the Welsh (*Gwynedd CC v Jones* [1986] I.C.R. 833).

(f) Both the Scots and the English are covered by the RRA by reference to "national origins" but not by "ethnic origins" (*Northern Joint Police Board v Power* [1997], *Boyce v British Airways* [1997]).

Positive discrimination

There is a difference between positive action and positive discrimination. Examples of positive action would be when an organisation seeks to promote applications for recruitment from certain, perhaps under-represented, sectors of society, *e.g.* ethnic minorities; or when a company actively encourages sections of its workforce, perhaps women, to attend training courses and seek promotions to positions in which they are under-represented. Such positive action is quite lawful, as long as the actual selection is made on merit and not on the basis of sex or origin.

Positive discrimination, for example restricting applications for a particular job to women only because women may be under-represented in that position or at that level, however, is generally not lawful. Discrimination in favour of one sex or any particular ethnic group will amount to discrimination against the other sex or other ethnic groups, and thus be contrary to the SDA or RRA. However, Art.2(4) of the Equal Treatment Directive allows for the introduction of "measures to promote equal opportunity for men and women, in particular by removing existing inequalities which affect women's opportunities". The ECJ have considered the extent to which this may allow positive discrimination, in two cases.

In the case of *Kalanke v Freie Hansestadt Bremen* [1995] I.R.L.R. 660 the court held that a rule which automatically gave priority to an equally qualified woman for a position in which women were under-represented, was contrary to the Equal Treatment Directive and would not fall within Art.2(4) of the Directive.

In the later case of *Marschall v Land Nordrhein Westfalen* [1998] I.R.L.R. 39 the ECJ appear to have adopted a different approach, stating that such a rule may not breach the Equal Treatment Directive if there is a guarantee that all candidates will be subject to an objective assessment which takes into account all the factors specific to the individual candidate, and the criteria used in the assessment are not in themselves discriminatory. It may be argued that the reasoning in *Marschall* is, in itself, self defeating; but it perhaps reflects a wider current European view that some positive discrimination in certain circumstances may not be harmful.

Under the Treaty of Amsterdam, amendments to Art.141 allow member states to adopt measures which provide for "specific advantages" to an under-represented sex in order to achieve full equality in practice. Such measures must therefore amount to positive discrimination, and indicate a pragmatic approach by the EU in seeking to achieve equality between men and women.

Sexual Orientation

The Court of Appeal in *R. v Ministry of Defence, Ex p. Smith* [1996] 1 All E.R. 257 stated that the legislation was aimed at gender discrimination, not orientation discrimination. In the case of *Smith v Gardner Merchant Ltd* [1998] I.R.L.R. 510 the Court of Appeal held that the SDA would apply in the case of a male homosexual harassed because of his sexual orientation if it could be shown that a female homosexual would not have been similarly treated—in other words if his treatment was because he was a man.

A similar approach was adopted by the Court of Sessions in the Scottish case of *MacDonald v Ministry of Defence* [2001] S.L.T. 819, where it was noted that although Mr MacDonald may have a remedy under the HRA 1998, the SDA 1975 is not presently concerned with issues of sexual orientation. On this issue two further points may be relevant; firstly, permission has recently been granted for an appeal to the House of Lords in the case of *Pearce v Mayfield Secondary School* [2000] I.R.L.R. 548 on the question of sexual orientation, and secondly, a new right not to be discriminated against on the grounds of sexual orientation is due to be introduced in 2003.

However, the law concerning transsexuals, those who have undergone, or intend to undergo gender reassignment is clearer. The ECJ in *P v S and Cornwall CC* [1996] I.R.L.R. 445 ruled that the Equal Treatment Directive would apply in such situations. Likewise, the EAT decision in *Chessington World of Adventure v Reed* [1998] I.R.L.R. 56 makes it clear that the SDA will apply in the case of discrimination against transsexuals. This has since been covered by legislation; SI 1999/1102 amending the SDA to specifically include discrimination on the grounds of gender reassignment, in so far as the applicant "intends to undergo, is undergoing or has undergone gender reassignment" (s.2A(1) of the SDA 1975).

Under both the SDA and the RRA there are three forms of discrimination: direct discrimination, indirect discrimination and victimisation.

Direct discrimination

A person discriminates against another if on the grounds of the other's sex or race the person treats the other less favourably than they treat or would treat other persons of a different sex or race (s.1 of the SDA 1975 and s.1 of the RRA 1976).

Case law has defined this as the "but for" test—would the victim have been treated differently but for his/her sex or race? (*James v Eastleigh Borough Council* [1990] I.R.L.R. 288.)

The motive for the discrimination is irrelevant (*James v Eastleigh*), thus direct discrimination brought about by good intentions or even unintentionally is still discrimination for the purposes of both Acts.

Segregation on racial grounds constitutes direct discrimination (s.1(2) of the RRA 1976), but allowing segregation to occur is apparently not actionable (*Pel Ltd v Modgill* [1980] I.R.L.R. 142).

There is case law to suggest that the *de minimis* rule should apply to discrimination, that is, if the act complained of is trivial, it need not constitute actionable discrimination (*Peake v Automotive Products* [1978] Q.B. 233). However, in recent years the courts have been reluctant to accept, let alone extend, this principle in practice.

In 2001 the Sex Discrimination (Indirect Discrimination and Burden of Proof) Regulations 2001 (SI 2001/2660) came into force. The effect is that it is no longer necessary for the complainant to prove their case, merely to establish the facts of the complaint. The burden of proof then moves to the person alleged to have discriminated, to rebut the presumption of discrimination. If they are not able to do so, the tribunal should then find discrimination.

Harassment

There are no provisions under either the SDA or the RRA to specifically deal with sexual or racial harassment. Indeed the term "harassment" is not used in either Act. However, the courts have held that harassment is a form of direct discrimination.

Harassment has been defined (in the case of sexual harassment) as "conduct of a sexual nature which is imposed by the perpetrator on an unwilling victim, and which the victim finds offensive" (IRLIB 3/4/90), and:

> "sexual harassment means unwanted conduct of a sexual nature, or other conduct based on sex affecting the dignity of women and men at work. This can include unwelcome physical, verbal or non-verbal conduct" (92/131/EEC).

However, case law has refined and amended these definitions somewhat:

(a) treatment of a particular kind, based on the sex of the victim, which would not have been used against an equally disliked member of the opposite sex (*Porcelli v Strathclyde RC* [1986] I.R.L.R. 134);
(b) it would be no defence that a person of the opposite sex to the victim would have been treated in a similar way (*British Telecommunications Plc v Williams* [1997] I.R.L.R. 668);
(c) a single act, if sufficiently serious, may constitute harassment (*Bracebridge Engineering Ltd v Darby* [1990] I.R.L.R. 3);
(d) a single verbal comment, if sufficiently serious, may constitute harassment (*In Situ Cleaning Co Ltd v Heads* [1995] I.R.L.R. 4);

and in view of the above, a better definition of harassment may now be "unwanted physical or verbal conduct directed against an individual on account of his or her sex or race".

Two further issues remain to be considered on this topic.

Firstly, s.6 of the SDA 1975 and s.4 of the RRA 1976 both state that the discrimination must subject the victim to either dismissal or "any other detriment". In the case of *De Souza v Automobile Association* [1986] I.R.L.R. 103, the Court of Appeal held that to prove racial harassment it was not sufficient to racially insult a coloured employee, even if that insult caused him distress, it would be necessary to prove that the employee was subjected to some "other detriment". Again, in the case of *Snowball v Gardner Merchant Ltd* [1987] I.C.R. 719, the EAT allowed evidence to be admitted to show that due to the victim's attitude towards sexual matters, the harassment may not in itself have caused a detriment. However, the later case of *In Situ Cleaning Co Ltd v Heads* doubts this line of reasoning by stating that detriment means no more than disadvantage, and thus the harassment itself becomes the detriment.

The second issue to be considered is that of the comparator. Unlike a claim for equal pay, an action for discrimination does not require that the complainant identifies an actual comparator. In all but one situation it is sufficient to apply the "but for" test and compare the action taken against the complainant with the action that would have been taken against a hypothetical comparator.

The one situation which is the exception is that of pregnancy and childbirth. Previously the courts had considered that the proper comparator for a pregnant woman should be a sick man. However, the ECJ in the case of *Webb v EMO Air Cargo Ltd* [1994] I.R.L.R. 482 held that "pregnancy is not in any way comparable with a pathological condition", thus there is no requirement for a comparator, either real or hypothetical. The ECJ also held that discrimination on the grounds of pregnancy amounted to direct discrimination.

A note of caution was however sounded by the House of Lords when the case was returned from the ECJ; Lord Keith did suggest that the dismissal of a pregnant woman may not be unlawful if the employee had been hired on a fixed-term contract, rather than on an open ended, ongoing basis. Lord Keith's reasoning appears to be that in such a situation the woman would not be dismissed on account of the pregnancy, but because of her unavailability to complete the contract for which she was engaged. In the case of *Carunana v Manchester Airport Plc* [1996] I.R.L.R. 378, the court chose to treat this exception as applying only where the woman would not be available for any part of the contract.

Victimisation

Victimisation occurs when an employer takes action amounting to discrimination against an employee, because the employee has brought proceedings, given evidence, or done anything under SDA, RRA, EqPA, or ss.62–65 of the Pensions Act 1995, or intends to do so (s.4 of the SDA 1975, s.2 of the RRA 1976). For an example see the case of *Aziz v Trinity Street Taxis Ltd* [1988] I.C.R. 534. The later case of *Nagarajan v London Regional Transport* [1999] I.R.L.R. 572 makes it clear that it is not necessary that the respondent acted with the intention of victimising, it is sufficient that they did the act complained of and that the act was an important cause of the decision.

Indirect Discrimination

Indirect discrimination is defined in s.1(1)(b) of the SDA 1975 and s.1(1)(b) of the RRA 1976 as applying a requirement or condition to all employees or potential employees, but the proportion of any particular sex or race who can comply with the condition is considerably smaller than the proportion of those from outside that sex or race who can comply, and the employer cannot justify that requirement, and the complainants inability to comply with the requirement is to their detriment.

The phrase "can comply" was considered in the case of *Mandla v Dowell Lee* [1983] I.C.R. 385, where Lord Fraser was of the opinion that it should not be given its literal meaning, *i.e.*. "can physically", but should be taken to mean "can in practice" or "can consistently with the customs and cultural conditions of the racial group". Thus an advertisement for a "bearded accounts clerk" would *prima facie* constitute indirect sex discrimination.

Examples of indirect discrimination have included:

(a) Discrimination against part-time workers, the majority of whom are women (*R. v Secretary of State for Employment, Ex p. EOC* [1994] 2 W.L.R. 409, which resulted in the removal of hour thresholds for certain employment rights by SI 1995/31).

(b) An age restriction of "must be between 17–28" was indirectly discriminatory against women because of family commitments (*Price v Civil Service Commission* [1978] I.C.R. 27.

(c) A rule that the successful candidate should not have young children was held to be indirectly discriminatory against women (*Thorndyke v Bell Fruit Ltd* [1979] I.R.L.R. 1).

(d) A contractual requirement to work full-time may be indirectly discriminatory against women (*Home Office v Holmes* [1984] I.C.R. 678, although see the later case of *Greater Glasgow Health Board v Carey* [1987] I.R.L.R. 484).

(e) The inclusion of a mobility clause in the employment contract may be discriminatory against women (*Meade-Hill v British Council* [1995] I.R.L.R. 478).

Pool of Comparators

In order to prove indirect discrimination it is necessary to show that the proportion of persons to which the complainant belongs who cannot comply with the imposed requirement is considerably smaller than the proportion of persons from outside the complainants group who can comply. Thus it is necessary to identify a pool of comparators.

The Court of Appeal in *Jones v University of Manchester* [1993] I.C.R. 474 warned against sub-dividing or otherwise manipulating the pool in order to bring about a particular result. It held that the relevant pool is the number of persons referred to in the legislation, *i.e.* the number of persons to whom the requirement has been or would be applied to by the employer.

Generally a monetary award will not be made against an employer in cases of unintentional indirect discrimination.

Dress codes

Whilst on the one hand the employer may issue rules regarding dress and uniform, and whilst these rules will normally form part of the work rules—breach of which may put an employee in breach of the employment contract—on the other hand, the rules themselves must not contravene discrimination laws.

In terms of sex discrimination the courts have adopted the approach that dress rules will not normally breach discrimination law if they apply a similar standard of conventionality to both men and women (*Smith v Safeway Plc* [1996] I.R.L.R. 456). Case law concerning racial discrimination is not quite so straightforward. Each case must be considered on its own facts and merits: in one case a ban on beards was not held to be unlawful discrimination against Sikhs (*Singh v Rowntree Mackintosh Ltd* [1979] I.R.L.R. 199), whereas in another case a Sikh woman dismissed for carrying a dagger contrary to the employer's work rules was unlawfully discriminated against (*Kaur v Butcher & Baker Foods Ltd* case 1304563/97).

Vicarious Liability

An employer may normally be held vicariously liable for acts committed by their employees in the course of their employment (s.41 of the SDA 1975, s.32 of the RRA 1976).

Under earlier case law, it was possible for an employer to avoid liability by arguing that it was no part of the employees job or duty to commit the acts complained of, and consequently, such acts were not committed in the course of employment (see *Irving v Post Office* [1987] I.R.L.R. 289).

However, the Court of Appeal in *Jones v Tower Boot Co Ltd* [1997] I.R.L.R. 168 rejected this approach, stating that the restrictive tortious definition of "in the course of employment" should not apply to cases of discrimination, but that the words should be given the broader definition a layman would apply to them. This purposive approach has been followed in the case of *Chief Constable of the Lincolnshire Police v Stubbs* [1999] I.R.L.R. 81, where the EAT held that, since work related social functions are an extension of employment, a male police officer who sexually harassed a female colleague at both an after work gathering and at an organised leaving party was acting "in the course of his employment".

The principles of vicarious liability in discrimination cases have also been extended by the EAT decision in *Burton and Rhule v De Vere Hotels* [1996] I.R.L.R. 596, in which it was held that an employer "subjects" an employee to the detriment of harassment when, in circumstances which he can control, he causes or permits the discrimination or harassment to take place.

CASE EXAMPLE

Burton and Rhule v De Vere Hotels [1996] I.R.L.R. 596

A function room was hired to a third party who booked the comedian Bernard Manning as guest speaker. During Manning's speech, which contained—perhaps not surprisingly—an amount of racially and sexually offensive material, he saw the two applicants, Afro-Caribbean waitresses, and made racially and sexually offensive remarks both to them and about them. They complained to the hotel management, their employer, who moved them away from working in that location. They then brought an action against their employer for racial harassment.

Held: Finding for the applicants, the EAT stated that:

> "an employer subjects an employee to the detriment of racial harassment if he causes or permits the racial harassment to occur in circumstances in which he can control whether it happens or not." *per* Smith J.

Commentary: The EAT was faced with a potentially difficult situation here—Manning was not an employee of the hotel, nor was there any contractual relationship between them, nor perhaps could the hotel be said to be responsible for Manning's actions. Although the hotel apparently acted reasonably by moving the waitresses, this was not enough. The EAT held that the hotel should have given thought to the risk of the event, and having identified the risk, acted on it to protect its staff.

The EAT also considered and distinguished the scenario of an employer foreseeing the real possibility of racial harassment towards its employees, but not being in a position to prevent it, *e.g.* bus conductor, etc.; also the scenario where an employer could not foresee the harassment, even though he has control over the situation. According to the EAT neither of these would apply in the present case; the harassment was foreseeable and the hotel did have control over the situation, thus they must accept responsibility.

Defences

It is a complete defence under s.7 of the SDA 1975 and s.5 of the RRA 1976 to a complaint of sexual or racial discrimination that the discrimination occurred where sex or race is a genuine occupational qualification.

The courts have tended to interpret the words "genuine occupational qualification" strictly, some examples are:

(a) For reasons of authenticity in dramatic performances (s.7(2)(a) of the SDA 1975);

(b) For reasons of authenticity where food or drink is pro-vided (s.5(2)(c) of the RRA 1976, *e.g.* a Chinese waiter/ess in a Chinese restaurant);

(c) The refusal to employ a female assistant in a menswear shop was held to be unlawful, since any intimate contact with customers could be undertaken by other male staff (*Wylie v Dee & Co (Menswear) Ltd* [1978] I.R.L.R. 103); and

(d) The refusal to employ a male assistant in a women's dress shop was held to be unlawful, since any intimate contact with customers could have been performed by other female staff (*Etam plc v Rowan*[1989] I.R.L.R. 150).

The best defence for an employer is that they have in place a comprehensive and effective equal opportunities policy—but such a policy must be properly promulgated and enforced among the workforce (*Balgobin v London Borough of Tower Hamlets* [1987] I.R.L.R. 401).

Remedies

Anyone who has suffered an act of sex or race discrimination has the right to make a complaint to an employment tribunal within three months of the occurrence of the act complained of (s.76(1) of the SDA 1975, s.68(1) of the RRA 1976), but the tribunal has the power to extend the time limit if it considers that it is just and equitable to do so (s.76(5) of the SDA 1975, s.68(6) of the RRA 1976).

The usual remedy sought is one of compensation. Compensation is payable according to the principles applicable in tort (s.65(1)(b) of the SdA 1975, s.56(1)(b) of the RRA 1976), and there is no upper limit to the amount of compensation that may be awarded.

A further remedy lies within s.65(1)(c) of the SDA 1975 and s.56(1)(c) of the RRA 1976, whereby the tribunal may make a recommendation that the respondent take within a specified period action to remove from the complainant the adverse effect of the discrimination complained of. Failure by the respondent to comply would allow the tribunal to increase or make an order for compensation.

In specific instances, further remedies may be available.

Disability Discrimination

Under s.5(1) of the Disability Discrimination Act 1995 (DDA),

> "an employer discriminates against a disabled person if—
> (a) for a reason which relates to the disabled person's disability, he treats him less favourably than he treats or would treat others. . . and
> (b) he cannot show that the treatment in question is justified."

Disability is defined as being a physical or mental impairment which has a substantial and long-term adverse effect on the ability to carry out normal day-to-day activities (s.1(1) of the DDA 1995). Thus being diagnosed HIV positive would not in itself bring one within the protection of the Act; but once the condition had progressed to the extent that it affected one's ability to perform normal day-to-day activities, it may then be classified as a disability.

It should be noted that the Act applies only to companies employing 15 or more people (s.7(1) of the DDA 1995), and in the case of *Hardie v CD Northern Ltd* [2000] I.R.L.R. 87 the court refused to count workers belonging to an associate employer.

Section 6 of DDA imposes on an employer a duty to make reasonable adjustments to such things as premises, equipment, allocation of duties, working hours, time off, instructions, and provision of a reader or interpreter. In deciding what would constitute "reasonable" steps, regard may be had as to what is practicable, the financial or other costs, and the resources available to the particular employer (s.6(4) of the DDA 1995).

As yet, there is limited case law to fully interpret all the aspects of the law in this area. However, the following may be instructive:

(a) An employer should plan ahead and consider the needs of future disabled employees (*Williams v Channel 5 Engg Services Ltd* case 230136/97).

(b) A justification of health and safety grounds was accepted for the suspension of an epileptic employee (*Smith v Carpets Intl UK Ltd* case 1800507/97).

(c) In the case of an employee dismissed for absence brought about by their disability, the proper comparator was a non-disabled employee absent through illness for a similar length of time (*Clark v Novacold Ltd* [1998] I.R.L.R. 420).

(d) It may be unlawful to select an applicant for redundancy on account of their disability, even where the employer takes the view that they must retain the most flexible workforce in order to meet their obligations (*Morse v Wiltshire CC* [1998] I.R.L.R. 352).

(e) The duty to make adjustments does not extend to a duty to provide a carer for a disabled employee (*Kenny v Hampshire Constabulary* [1999] I.C.R. 27).

(f) The duty to make adjustments may only arise once an employer knows or could reasonably know of the worker's disability (*O'Neill v Symm & Co Ltd* [1998] I.R.L.R. 233), but see also *HJ Heinz Co Ltd v Kenrick* [2000] I.R.L.R. 144.

CASE EXAMPLE

Morse v Wiltshire CC **[1998] I.R.L.R. 352**

Mr Morse, a road worker with Wiltshire Council, suffered a 20 per cent disability which left him with limited movement in his right hand and leg; he also suffered from blackouts. When he returned to work he was unable to drive, operate power tools, or work on heights or near water when alone.

When a redundancy situation arose, the council took the view that its retained workforce must be flexible, and that all should be able to drive. Mr Morse was assessed as part of the redundancy selection procedure, and along with others he was selected for redundancy.

Mr Morse brought an action for disability discrimination, which was dismissed by the employment tribunal on the grounds that the employers could not have made adjustments to the job or working conditions to accommodate Mr Morse. He then appealed to the EAT.

Held: In a reserved judgement the appeal was allowed and remitted to a freshly constituted employment tribunal.

Commentary: The case is important, not particularly for its facts, but for the procedure laid down by the EAT.

An employment tribunal hearing a case of disability discrimination must go through a series of steps, as follows:

(a) The tribunal must decide whether the provisions of ss.6(1)–6(2) of the DDA 1995 impose a s.6(1) of the DDA 1995 duty on the employer in this particular situation.
(b) If such a duty is imposed, the tribunal must consider whether the employer has taken all such steps as are reasonable in the circumstances.
(c) The tribunal should then consider whether the employer could have taken any of the particular steps laid out in s.6(3) of the DDA 1995.
(d) At the same time the tribunal should consider the reasonableness of taking such steps, as detailed in s.6(4) of the DDA 1995.
(e) If the tribunal finds that the employer has failed to comply with a s.6 duty, it must then decide whether the employer's failure to comply is justified (s.5(2)(b) of the DDA 1995).
(f) The tribunal must apply an objective test, asking not only whether the employer's reason for the failure was reasonable, but also asking what possible steps the employer could have taken, before reaching its own decision on what steps were reasonable.

7. OTHER STATUTORY RIGHTS

NATIONAL MINIMUM WAGE ACT 1998

The National Minimum Wage Act 1998 (NWMA) was introduced to provide a basic minimum hourly rate of pay for all workers. Section 2(1) enables the Secretary of State to determine and amend the hourly rate at appropriate intervals. Two rates of pay are set; one for workers aged 20 years and over, and a lower one for those workers aged 18–20 years.

Scope of the Act

The Act applies to all workers, not merely employees, and includes agency workers (s.34 of the NWMA 1998) and home workers (s.35 of the NWMA 1998), but specific exclusions cover certain voluntary workers, members of the armed forces, prisoners and certain ship-board workers.

Rights under the Act

The Act affords to all of those covered the right to be paid the minimum wage, the right of access to wage records, and the right not to suffer detriment for asserting a right under the Act—the remedy being via a complaint to an Employment Tribunal. An employee who is dismissed for asserting a statutory right will be treated as having been unfairly dismissed (s.104 of the ERA 1996).

WORKING TIME REGULATIONS 1998

The Working Time Regulations 1998 are intended to implement the Working Time Directive 93/104 and parts of the Young Workers Directive 94/33.

Main Provisions

(a) A maximum working week of 48 hours, averaged over a 17-week period. It is possible for individuals to opt out of this restriction.

(b) Night workers to average no more than 8 hours work in each 24-hour period, calculated over a 17-week period. It is possible for individuals to opt out of this restriction.

(c) Certain night workers—those involved with heavy physical or mental strain, or whose work involves particular special hazards, may work only 8 hours in a 24-hour period, without exception.

(d) All night workers are entitled to a health assessment before being required to work nights, and regular check-ups thereafter.

(e) Adult workers are entitled to 1 day off per week, 11 continuous rest hours per day, and a minimum break of 20 minutes if the working day is 6 hours or more.

(f) Young workers (those over the minimum school leaving age, but under 18 years old) are entitled to 2 days off per week, 12 continuous rest hours per day, and a minimum break of 30 minutes if the working day is 4½ hours or more.

(g) Since November 23, 1999 all workers are entitled, after a 13-week qualifying period, to 4 weeks annual paid leave. Any provision within a contract claiming "there is no entitlement to paid holidays under this contract" have been held to be void (*The College of North East London v Leather*, EAT 30/11/01).

"Worker" is defined in the Regulations in the same way as s.230(3) of the ERA 1996, and includes both those working under a contract of employment (employees) and those working under any other contract to personally provide any work or service to another party, unless the other party's status under the contract is that of client or customer of any profession or business undertaking carried on by the individual.

The term "worker" also applies to apprentices, trainees and those on work experience programmes.

Almost certainly "worker" applies to casual workers, particularly following *Carmichael v National Power Plc* [1998] I.R.L.R. 301, but a recent Privy Council decision in *Chen Yuen v Royal Hong Kong Golf Club* [1998] I.C.R. 131 highlights an instance where, apparently and surprisingly, it was held that no contract of any sort was in existence between golf caddies and the golf club they "worked" for.

Agency workers are specifically included in the definition of "worker", by reg.36, the party responsible under the Regulations being the party who pays the agency worker—in most cases the employment agency.

Exclusions

Areas of activity excluded by the Regulations include:

(a) The transport industry. It has recently been held by the ECJ (*Bowden v Tuffnells Parcels Express Ltd* Case C-133/00) that the exclusion covers all workers within the transport industry—not merely mobile workers. However, the forthcoming Directive 2000/34 will restrict the exclusion of workers from industries such as road transport to mobile workers only.

(b) Junior doctors. Regulation 18(b) excludes all doctors under training.

(c) Work at sea; including fishing, shipping and offshore working.

(d) The Police and Armed Forces. The Regulations probably do not apply in most instances to the ambulance service, fire service, prison service, etc.

(e) Those with autonomous decision making powers as to the duration of their working time, *e.g.* managing executives, those working in family businesses, etc.

(f) Security work, requiring round-the-clock presence.

(g) Continuous production processes, including hospitals, prisons, etc., although the exclusion is dependent upon the worker's activities, rather than merely on the place of work.

(h) Seasonal industries, such as tourism, Christmas business, agricultural activities, *e.g.* fruit picking.

CASE EXAMPLE

Barber v RJB Mining UK Ltd **[1999] I.R.L.R. 308.**
Pit deputies and colliery overmen at a privatised colliery were being required to work in excess of 48 hours per week. The employer argued that the men were only being asked to work their normal hours and the Working Time Directive was not to be read as forming part of the employment contract.

Held: The Directive, and by implication the Regulations, are a mandatory requirement and apply to all contracts of employment.

Commentary: This is as would be expected, the importance of the case lies in the fact that it was the first to be brought under the new legislation.

MATERNITY RIGHTS

Dismissal on Pregnancy-Related Grounds

An employee will be regarded as unfairly dismissed if the reason or principal reason for her dismissal is that she is pregnant or any other reason connected with her pregnancy (s.99(1)(a) of the ERA 1996, and see by *Webb v EMO Air Cargo* [1995] I.R.L.R. 645).

An employee will also be regarded as being unfairly dismissed if during the period of her maternity leave she submits a doctor's certificate stating that due to illness she will be unable to return to work following the leave period, and she is dismissed for a reason connected with the birth within four weeks of the end of her maternity leave period (s.99(3) of the ERA 1996, and see *Brown v Rentokil Ltd* [1997] I.R.L.R. 445).

It has been held that dismissal on the grounds of a pregnancy related illness after the maternity leave ends may not constitute unfair dismissal (*Hertz v Aldi Marked K/S* [1991] I.R.L.R. 31). However, be aware of the more recent case of *Caledonia Bureau Investment & Property Ltd v Caffrey* [1998] I.R.L.R. 110, in which it was held by the EAT that a dismissal, which occurred after the maternity leave was over, for post-natal depression—a pregnancy-related illness—was for a reason connected with the pregnancy and therefore contrary to s.99(1) of the ERA 1996.

Maternity Leave

Legislation concerning provision of maternity leave is complex. Part VIII ERA, as amended by ERelA 1999, gives effect to the Pregnant Workers Directive (Directive 82/95) and provides for a minimum of 18 weeks maternity leave to all pregnant employees without the need for a minimum period of service. The leave may begin no earlier than the 11th week prior to the expected week of childbirth. During the maternity leave the employee is entitled to all the normal benefits which would have accrued under her contract, and, in the absence of any contractual right to pay, if she has a minimum of 26 weeks of continuous service, is entitled to statutory maternity pay.

If the employee has a minimum of one year's service at the beginning of the 11th week before childbirth, she has the right to return to work at any time up to 29 weeks after childbirth. She is entitled to return to work on terms no less favourable than she would have enjoyed had she not been absent.

There is provision within the EA 2002 for maternity leave to be increased to six months' paid and six months' unpaid for working mothers.

Time Off for Ante-Natal Care

A pregnant employee has a right under s.55 of the ERA 1996 to time off during the employer's working hours to keep an appointment to receive ante-natal care.

Statutory Maternity Pay

An employee with a minimum of 26 weeks continuous service is entitled to receive statutory maternity pay for the period of her statutory maternity leave. For the first six weeks it amounts to 90 per cent of her average weekly earnings, and for a further 12 weeks at a rate set by statute (SI 1986/1960).

CASE EXAMPLE

Webb v EMO Air Cargo (UK) Ltd [1995] I.R.L.R. 645
Mrs Webb had been hired by EMO Air Cargo, a small company employing 16 people, as a replacement for one of their staff who was absent on maternity leave. It was envisaged that Mrs Webb would continue to work with EMO once the maternity replacement period was over. Some two weeks after starting work, Mrs Webb discovered that she was pregnant. On learning of this, her employer dismissed her. Mrs Webb brought a claim to an employment tribunal alleging sex discrimination.

Held: The House of Lords made the following points:
Discrimination on the grounds of pregnancy is sex discrimination. There is no need for the applicant to compare herself to a "sick man". It is possible that the dismissal may have been held

to be a fair dismissal had Mrs Webb been appointed *only* on a fixed term contract (but see the case of *Carunana v Manchester Airport plc* [1996] I.R.L.R. 378).

Commentary: Although a similar case today may be brought under s.99 of the ERA 1996—dismissal on the grounds of pregnancy being automatically unfair—a sex discrimination claim may be advantageous because it would also cover the recruitment process, and also, unlike unfair dismissal claims, there is no upper limit on compensation awards for sex discrimination.

Paternity leave

The EA 2002 makes provision for those employees with 26 weeks continuous service to be entitled to a period of at least two weeks' paid paternity leave.

Adoption Leave

Under the EA 2002 both ordinary adoption leave and additional adoption leave, the periods of which are presently still to be decided, are to be made available to those employees with a minimum of 26 weeks qualifying service.

HUMAN RIGHTS ACT 1998

The HRA 1998 has created new, directly enforceable rights against public bodies and against quasi-public bodies undertaking public functions.

The Act does not however make European Convention on Human Rights (the Convention) rights directly enforceable against a private litigant—an individual or a private business or company.

What the Act does is to give effect to Convention rights by obliging courts to decide all cases compatibly with Convention rights—unless prevented from doing so by primary legislation (s.6 of the HRA 1998), by obliging courts wherever possible to interpret legislation in conformity with the Convention (s.3 of the HRA 1998), and by requiring courts to take account of Convention based case law (s.2 of the HRA 1998).

It is not yet at all clear what effect the Act will have in the area of Employment Law specifically.

Generally, if legislation is held to be incompatible with the Convention, procedures are in place whereby the government can implement fast-track legislation to remedy the situation. Certainly in areas of criminal law, particularly evidential rules, the Act is likely to have considerable long-term impact.

PUBLIC INTEREST DISCLOSURE ACT 1998

The purpose of the Act is to protect workers against action taken by their employers in cases where the worker "blows the whistle" on certain actions of his employer.

The Act protects a worker against dismissal, selection for redundancy or any other detriment, if the reason or principal reason for the action is that the worker has made a "protected disclosure".

The term "worker" is given an extended definition by the Act and includes:

(a) Those working under a contract of employment (s.230(3)(a) of the ERA 1996).

(b) Those working under a contract to personally or otherwise provide any work or services in a place that is not under the control of the individual—unless that other party is a client or customer of any profession or business carried out by the individual, *i.e.* unless the individual is genuinely running their own business, (s.230(3)(b) of the ERA 1996, as amended by PIDA).

(c) Agency workers, being those supplied or introduced by a third party (s.1 of the PIDA 1998).

(d) A person providing medical, dental, ophthalmic or pharmaceutical services in accordance with arrangements made by a Health Authority under ss.29, 35, 38 or 41 of the National Health Service Act 1977, or the equivalent in Scotland (s.1 of the PIDA 1998).

(e) A person being provided with training or work experience, unless under a contract of employment or as part of a course run by an educational establishment.

Qualifying Disclosure

A "qualifying disclosure" is defined in the Act as being a disclosure of information which the worker reasonably believes shows or tends to show:

(a) that a criminal offence has been, is being or is likely to be committed; or

(b) that a person has failed, is failing or is likely to fail to comply with a legal obligation; or

(c) that a miscarriage of justice has occurred, is occurring or is likely to occur; or

(d) that health and safety has been, is being or is likely to be endangered; or

(e) that the environment has been, is being or is likely to be damaged; or

(f) that information concerning any of the above has been, is being or is likely to be deliberately concealed.

It is immaterial whether the relevant failure occurs or would occur in the UK or elsewhere.

However, the disclosure is not a qualifying disclosure if the person making it commits an offence by making it; nor will it be a qualifying disclosure if the information is subject to legal professional privilege, and had been disclosed to the person in the course of obtaining legal advice.

Protected Disclosure

A qualifying disclosure will become a protected disclosure in the following circumstances:

(a) If the worker makes the disclosure to the employer, or to the person the worker reasonably believes is responsible for the relevant failure; or

(b) If the disclosure is made in the course of obtaining legal advice; or

(c) If the worker's employer is appointed by enactment by a Minister of the Crown, the disclosure is made in good faith to a Minister of the Crown; or

(d) If the disclosure is made in good faith to a person prescribed by the Secretary of State for the purpose of the Act.

A disclosure made to a person other than the employer or a prescribed person may also qualify as a protected disclosure if, but only if, the worker making the disclosure:

(a) Makes it in good faith;

(b) Reasonably believes it to be true;

(c) Does not make personal gain from the disclosure;

(d) Reasonably believes that he would be subject to some detriment if he makes the disclosure to his employer;

(e) Reasonably believes that relevant evidence would be concealed or destroyed if he makes the disclosure to his employer; and

(f) Has already disclosed the same information to his employer or to a prescribed person.

In deciding whether it is reasonable for the worker to make the disclosure, regard will be had to, amongst other issues:

(a) The identity of the person to whom the disclosure is made;

(b) The seriousness of the relevant failure;

(c) Whether the disclosure relates to a past, present or future failure;

(d) whether the disclosure breaches a duty of confidentiality owed by the employer to another person; and

(e) where the disclosure has already been made to the employer or a prescribed person, any action taken, or which should have been taken.

Exceptionally Serious Failures

In the case of an "exceptionally serious failure" regard need only be had to whether the worker makes the disclosure in good faith, believing it to be true, does not make personal gain from the disclosure, and in all the circumstances whether it was reasonable to make the disclosure, particularly in respect of the identity of the person to whom it was made.

FIXED-TERM EMPLOYEES (PREVENTION OF LESS FAVOUR-ABLE TREATMENT) REGULATIONS 2002

From October 1, 2002 these Regulations, brought in under the Employment Act 2002, oblige all employers to treat fixed-term employees no less favourably than comparable permanent employees. Fixed-term employees are those working under a contract for a specific fixed time, for a specific task, or a contract which will terminate upon the happening, or non-happening, of some future event. The Regulations also limit the use of successive fixed-term contracts to a maximum of four years, unless objective justification for further periods can be shown by the employer; this is designed to prevent employers avoiding such employment rights as redundancy entitlements by the use of a series of fixed-term appointments.

8. HEALTH AND SAFETY

The aim of health and safety law is to prevent accidents occurring in the workplace. The enforcement of health and safety legislation differs from most other areas of employment law in that breach of a health and safety statute usually results in criminal liability. However, this does not prevent the injured party from pursuing a claim for damages in the event of an accident.

Sources of Health and Safety Law

The main sources of health and safety law in England and Wales are the common law, statute and European Legislation.

Much of the common law regarding health and safety as it relates to the individual employee is contained in the employer's implied term of duty of care. The major consolidating domestic legislation is the Health and Safety at Work Act 1974 (HSWA), which over the years has been supported and complimented by other legislation, including input from the EC.

The Treaty of Rome includes Art.118A, which states:

> "The Member States shall pay particular attention to encouraging improvements, especially in the working environment, as regards the health and safety of workers, and shall set as their objective the harmonisation of conditions in this area, while maintaining the improvements."

One outcome of this has been the adoption of a Directive to encourage improvements in health and safety in the field of employment—the "Framework Directive"—Directive 89/391.

COMMON LAW

At common law the basis of the employer's duty towards his employees arises from the existence of the contract of employment. There is an implied term in the contract that the employer will take reasonable care to ensure the safety of his employees. Breach of this duty will amount to a breach of contract, and may allow the employee to leave, claim constructive dismissal and bring an action for unfair dismissal (see Unfair Dismissal).

In the case of injury to the employee however, there is normally no advantage to suing in contract, and most claims are brought in the tort of negligence (*Donoghue v Stevenson* [1932] A.C. 562).

The employer's liability will arise in one of two ways. He will be directly responsible for his own actions or omissions which amount to negligence; he may also be responsible for the negligent actions or omissions of other employees, through the doctrine of vicarious liability.

Employer's Direct Liability

Under the common law it is necessary to ask two questions:

(a) Was the injured party someone the employer should have reasonably foreseen would be likely to have been injured if the work had not been carried out properly?
(b) In all the circumstances did the employer attain the standard of care expected from a reasonable employer?

The injured party must show three things:

(a) that the employer owed a duty of care;
(b) that there was a breach of that duty; and
(c) that the breach was the cause of the injury.

Duty of Care

The duty of the employer is owed to the employee as an individual (*Paris v Stepney Borough Council* [1951] A.C. 376), and consequently a higher standard of care may be owed to some employees than to others (*James v Hepworth & Grandage Ltd* [1968] 1 Q.B. 94). The duty is owed by the employer, and may not be delegated—although the performance of the duty may be (*Wilsons and Clyde Coal Co Ltd v English* [1938] A.C. 57).

The duty is generally divided into four areas:

(a) Safe Plant and Equipment–reasonable steps should be taken by the employer to provide and maintain safe plant and equipment.

CASE EXAMPLE

Bradford v Robinson Rentals **[1967] 1 All E.R. 267**
In a particularly cold spell an employee was instructed to make a delivery involving a round trip of some 400 miles, in a van which had no heating and badly fitting windows. He suffered frostbite and brought an action against his employer.

Held: The employer was liable for failing to provide suitable and safe plant and equipment.

(b) Safe Place of Work–the employer has a duty to take reasonable steps to ensure that the workplace is safe, not only for his employees, but also for anyone else who may use the premises (Occupiers Liability Act 1957 and 1984).

CASE EXAMPLE

Latimer v AEC Ltd **[1953] A.C. 643**
Rain had flooded a factory floor, which had become slippery with a mixture of oil and water. Sawdust was laid over most of the floor, but there was not sufficient sawdust to cover the entire floor. An employee slipped on part of the untreated floor and was injured.

Held: The employer was held not liable. Reasonable precautions had been taken, and the court held that the danger was not sufficient to warrant closing the factory entirely.

(c) Safe System of Work–the employer has a duty to ensure that the methods used to undertake the work are safe.

This includes the system, training, supervision, protective clothing, warnings, etc.

The employer is responsible for ensuring that the system is carried out, and must bear in mind that employees may be forgetful or lazy, however the employer may not be liable in cases of disobedience.

CASE EXAMPLE

McWilliams v Sir William Arrol & Co Ltd **[1962] 1 All E.R. 623**
Steel erectors working on a building site were provided with safety belts, which they chose not to wear. The belts were removed to another site, and shortly afterwards one of the employees on the first site fell and was killed.

Held: The employer was not held liable for the death, as it was shown that the employees had always chosen not to wear them (see also the issue of Causation).

(d) Provision of Competent Fellow Employees–the employer has a duty to recruit and train competent fellow employees; this may include the dismissal of incompetent workers.

CASE EXAMPLE

Hudson v Ridge Manufacturing Co Ltd **[1957] 2 Q.B. 348**
For a number of years an employee had played practical jokes including tripping fellow employees. On one occasion an employee sustained a serious injury, and brought an action against the employer.

Held: The employer was aware of the horseplay over a number of years but had taken no action to stop it; thus they were held liable.

Breach of Duty

The plaintiff must show that the employer's actions fell below the standard expected of a reasonable employer.

Obviously, the greater the risk, the greater the care required; and the more likely the risk, the more necessary the care. In deciding how a reasonable employer would have acted in a given situation, the court will take into account the cost of the action necessary (see *Latimer v AEC Ltd* where the only alternative to the employer would have been to close the factory entirely).

Breach as the Cause of the Injury

The breach must be the cause of the injury. See, *e.g. McWilliams v Sir William Arrol & Co Ltd*, where even though the employer was in breach of his duty by removing the safety belts, evidence showed that even if they had been present the employees would not have used them. Thus the employer's breach was held not to be the cause of the injury.

The normal tort rules of remoteness apply, thus if the employer is negligent in respect of a foreseeable type of injury he will be liable for all loss of that type arising from his action.

Defences

There are two main defences available:

(a) Contributory negligence on the part of the employee, in which case the court has discretion under the Law Reform (Contributory Negligence) Act 1945 to reduce proportionally the damages payable.

(b) Consent to the risk by the employee (*volenti non fit injuria*). This is a complete defence, but the courts are aware that in reality employees very rarely give real consent to injury.

CASE EXAMPLE

ICI Ltd v Shatwell [1965] A.C. 656
Two shot-firers deliberately broke both statutory regulations and the employer's instructions, resulting in injury to both of

them. One of them then brought an action against the employer on the basis of their vicarious liability for the actions of the other shot-firer.

Held: The employer was not liable, the complete defence of *volenti non fit injuria* succeeded.

Employer's Indirect Liability

If a third party is injured due to the negligence of an employee, the employer may be liable under the doctrine of vicarious liability, but only if the employee is acting in the course of his employment.

The concept of "in the course of employment" as used in tort is no longer the same as is used in cases of discrimination (see Chapter "Discrimination"). In discrimination cases the courts now interpret the phrase in the way that a layman would understand it, following the Court of Appeal decision in *Jones v Tower Boot Co Ltd*. In tort cases, however, the phrase is still interpreted more strictly, and is taken generally to mean that the employer will only be vicariously liable for the actions of his employees if the actions are carried out with the authority of the employer; although it is necessary to bear in mind the House of Lords ruling in *Lister v Hesley Hall Ltd* [2001] I.R.L.R. 472, which in at least some scenarios redefines and broadens the common law test.

CASE EXAMPLE

Kay v ITW Ltd **[1968] 1 Q.B. 140**
A fork-lift truck driver found that his way was blocked by a lorry. Although he had no specific instruction to do so, he moved the lorry himself, and in so doing injured another employee.

Held: The employer was held to be vicariously liable, since the action was not so extreme as to take it outside of his normal activities.

Hilton v Thomas Burton Ltd **[1961] 1 W.L.R. 705**
An employee made use of a firm's van to drive to a cafe on an unauthorised work break. In so doing he knocked down and killed a fellow worker.

Held: Although the employee had the general permission of the employer to drive the van, at the time of the incident he was acting outside the course of his employment. Thus the employer was not liable.

The Tort of Breach of Statutory Duty

There is no automatic presumption that all breaches of statutory duties are actionable in the civil court (*Cutler v Wandsworth Stadium Ltd* [1949] A.C. 398). Many recent statutes make clear that a breach will give rise to an action for breach of statutory duty, *e.g.* s.47(2) of the HSWA 1974, but the issue is far less clear with older legislation.

There are four elements to the tort:

(a) the plaintiff must show that he is within the class of person the legislation was designed to protect;
(b) that the injury sustained is of a type that the legislation was intended to prevent;
(c) that the company, the defendant, is actually in breach of the duty; and
(d) the question of causation must be satisfied.

STATUTE

The main and most important piece of domestic legislation is the Health and Safety at Work Act 1974 (HSWA). It is a complex and detailed piece of legislation, which when introduced had far reaching consequences for health and safety in the workplace.

The Act imposes a duty on employees to act reasonably. Sections 7 and 8 state that the employee should take reasonable care, both for his own safety and for the safety of others. The employee is also under a duty to co-operate with the employer in carrying out the Health and Safety policy, which each employer must prepare under s.2(3) of the HSWA 1974.

The main thrust of the Act, however, is aimed at the employer. Section 2 states that it is the duty of every employer to ensure, so far as is reasonably practicable, the health, safety and welfare at work of all his employees, including the maintenance of safe systems of work, safe place of work, safe working environment and adequate training.

"So far as is reasonably practicable" does not mean that the employer has an absolute duty to eliminate all risks.

CASE EXAMPLE

West Bromwich Building Society v Townsend **[1983] I.C.R. 257** A Health and Safety Executive (HSE) inspector alleged that the employer had not taken reasonable steps to ensure the protection of its staff by failing to erect bandit screens on its counters.

Held: Since the danger of attack was relatively slight, the staff had all been trained not to resist attack, and the screens would appear contrary to the society's customer friendly image, the court held that the society had done everything reasonably practicable.

Additionally, the Act provides for:

(a) The establishment of the Health and Safety Commission, an advisory body appointed by the Secretary of State to secure the health, safety and welfare of workers. It also proposes new legislation and standards.
(b) The establishment of a unified enforcement procedure under the HSE, which has a staff of over 4,500 including inspectors, policy advisors, technical and medical experts. The HSE also publishes a number of Approved Codes of Practice and Guidance Notes.

If an HSE inspector is of the opinion that an employer is contravening the Act, ss.21 and 22 of the HSWA 1974 give him the power to issue an improvement notice requiring that the problem be remedied, or in the case of serious danger, a prohibition notice requiring that an activity be discontinued until the situation is remedied.

Furthermore, the Act is an enabling Act, and has been used to implement EC Directives.

EC Framework Directive

EC Directive 89/391 concerning the harmonisation of health and safety legislation in Europe, along with six other directives concerning specific subjects, were implemented by a series of regulations introduced at the beginning of 1993.

(a) Management of health and safety at work regulations 1992.
  The framework regulations, imposing a duty on employers to carry out risk assessment measures, put into practice preventative measures, and nominate health and safety representatives.
(b) Provision and Use of Work Equipment Regulations 1992.
(c) Manual Handling Operations Regulations 1992.
(d) Workplace (Health, Safety and Welfare) Regulations 1992.
  Replacing much existing legislation concerning work environment, provision of workplace facilities, etc.
(e) Personal Protective Equipment at Work Regulations 1992.
(f) Health and Safety (Display Screen Equipment) Regulations 1992.

CASE EXAMPLE

Stark v The Post Office [2000] I.C.R. 1013
Mr Stark worked for the Post Office as a postman delivering letters, for which purpose the Post Office provided him with a bicycle. One day the front brake on the bicycle broke, causing the wheel to jam and Mr Stark to be thrown to the floor, where he sustained injuries. Both parties accepted that a prior examination of the bicycle would not have revealed the defect, and consequently there was no way in which the employer could have had prior warning of the accident. However, it was argued for Mr Stark that reg.6 of the Provision and Use of Work Equipment Regulations 1992 imposed an absolute obligation on the employer to ensure that the equipment was maintained in good repair.

Held: Although the Directives (Work Equipment Directive 89/655 and Framework Directive 89/391) may be read as laying down a less than absolute duty, the same could not be said of the Regulations, which had been drafted so as to impose an absolute duty on the employer.

Commentary: The Regulations thus impose an absolute, strict liability on the employer, which is, of course, a far higher level of duty than is imposed by common law.

9. TERMINATION OF EMPLOYMENT

There are three main methods by which employment may be terminated: termination by way of contract, termination in breach of contract, and termination by methods external to the contract.

Termination By Way of Contract

Every contract of employment will contain as a term of the contract details of how the contract may be lawfully determined by either party. Except in certain circumstances this will involve one party giving notice to the other party. Such notice period should be no less than the statutory minimum laid down in s.86 of the ERA 1996.

Under s.86 minimum notice periods are as follows:

(a) employed for between one month and two years—one week's notice;
(b) employed for between two and twelve years—one week for each year of employment; or
(c) employed for over twelve years—twelve weeks' notice.

These will apply where either no notice period is quoted in the contract, or the notice period stated in the contract is less than this. If the contractual notice period is longer, the longer period will apply.

It is, of course, possible for the employee to determine the contract for any reason by giving the required amount of notice. Failure to give such notice would allow the employer to bring an action for breach of contract, but in practice and for a number of reasons this is rarely done.

Statute has imposed certain restrictions and obligations on the part of the employer when seeking to determine the employment contract and so dismiss the employee. Not only does the employee have the right to certain minimum notice periods (s.86 of the ERA 1996), there is also a right not to be unfairly dismissed (s.94 of the ERA 1996), and a right to compensation if the reason for dismissal is redundancy (s.135 of the ERA 1996).

Termination in Breach of Contract

If the contract of employment is terminated by the employer—in other words if the employee is dismissed—in circumstances or for reasons outside of the contractual terms, the dismissal will constitute a breach of contract by the employer. This will allow the employee in many cases to bring an action for either **wrongful dismissal** or **unfair dismissal** (see Chapters 10 and 11).

In theory, if the employee was to terminate the contract in circumstances or for reasons outside of the contractual terms, this would allow the employer to bring an action for breach of contract. However, in practice this very rarely happens. Most companies would not wish to sue an ex-employee for damages in such circumstances, partly because the chances of financial success are in reality small, and partly because such action would probably give rise to adverse publicity.

A further factor is that s.236 of the Trade Union and Labour Relations (Consolidation) Act 1992 states:

> "No court shall, whether by way of—
>
> (a) an order for specific performance or specific implement of a contract of employment, or
> (b) an injunction or interdict restraining a breach or threatened breach of such a contract,
>
> compel an employee to do any work or attend at any place for the doing of any work."

Thus the courts may not enforce a contract of employment against an employee so as to force the employee either to work or to attend for work. For a narrow but apparently just interpretation of this law, see the case of *Evening Standard v Henderson* [1987] I.C.R. 588.

Termination by Methods External to the Contract

Since in many respects the employment contract is similar to any other contract, the doctrine of frustration of contract applies to it.

Frustration may be defined as an act external to the contract which is not caused by the fault of either party, and which was not foreseen by the parties to the contract (and thus not planned for within the contract), which has the effect of fundamentally altering the contract, or making it impossible to perform.

The effect of frustration on the contract of employment is that the contract is held to be immediately terminated without a dismissal taking place. Since, in law, no dismissal has taken place, the ex-employee will be unable to claim either wrongful dismissal or unfair dismissal.

In order to decide whether the employment contract has been frustrated, and to an extent to mitigate the harshness to the employee in such situations, a number of factors for consideration were laid down in the case of *Egg Stores (Stamford Hill) Ltd v Leibovici* [1977] I.C.R. 260, including length of previous employment, nature of the job, nature and effect of the disabling event, the requirement for a replacement, whether a reasonable employer could be expected to wait any longer, etc.

Examples of frustration of the contract of employment include:

(a) Imposition of a prison sentence (*FC Shepherd & Co Ltd v Jerrom* [1986] I.R.L.R. 358). It has been argued that the imposition of a prison sentence must amount to the fault of the employee, thus it cannot constitute frustration. Although there is some logic in this, if it were accepted it would mean that an employee sentenced to imprisonment would be able to sue for wrongful dismissal if given no notice period, or even for unfair dismissal; whilst an employee whose contract was frustrated through illness would have no such recourse. This would give a situation in which the employee at fault is in a better position than the employee whose contract is terminated through no fault of their own. The court in *Shepherd v Jerrom* considered such a situation to be "an affront to common sense", and therefore held that imprisonment could lead to frustration.

(b) Medical evidence that the worker could probably never work again (*Notcutt v Universal Equipment Co Ltd* [1986] I.R.L.R. 218). In cases of long term sickness, the court will consider such factors as how long the employee is expected to be absent, the need of the employer to obtain a replacement, how long the employee has been employed, the provision of sick pay within the contract, etc. Long term absence from work will not automatically constitute frustration.

The courts are unwilling to find frustration of employment contracts too readily; in *Williams v Watson Luxury Coaches Ltd* [1990] I.R.L.R. 164 it was stated that frustration in employment would be a rare occurrence, and the doctrine should be severely limited.

Death of the Employer

At common law the death of the employer would have the effect of terminating the contract of employment without giving rise to a dismissal. In similar circumstances, however, statute would deem a dismissal to have taken place (s.136(5) of the ERA 1996).

---

10. WRONGFUL DISMISSAL

The Basic Position

An action for wrongful dismissal is a common law action for damages to compensate the ex-employee for losses suffered for the wrongful termination of the employment contract. Generally this will only amount to monies to which the employee would have been contractually entitled had the contract been lawfully terminated, in effect, monies in lieu of notice.

Normally such damages will be limited to either wages for the minimum statutory notice period, or the notice period stipulated by the contract, whichever is the longer. The damages represent only the basic wages and other contractual entitlements; there is no entitlement to any discretionary payments, *e.g.* bonus or salary increases, etc.

Thus, an action for wrongful dismissal concerns only whether the correct contractual notice period has been given; as such, the reason for the dismissal is irrelevant (*Addis v Gramophone Co Ltd* [1909] A.C. 488). Remember, of course, that in a number of circumstances an employer may summarily dismiss an employee quite lawfully, *e.g.* for gross misconduct (see *Sinclair v Neighbour* [1967] 2 Q.B. 279, *Pepper v Webb* [1969] 1 W.L.R. 514 *Cf. Wilson v Racher* [1974] I.C.R. 428).

Other Developments

In most circumstances, the employer will be able to discharge their obligations under the contract by paying money in lieu of notice, and not requiring or not allowing the employee to work a notice period. There are, however, some situations where such action may in itself constitute a separate breach of contract, *e.g.* actors or others whose work requires them to be exposed or displayed to the public. In such cases the courts have been prepared to award separate damages for damage to reputation (*Herbert Clayton & Jack Waller Ltd v Oliver* [1930] A.C. 209).

In the recent case of *Malik v BCCI SA* [1997] I.R.L.R. 462 the House of Lords held that where the manner of the dismissal constituted a breach of the contractual term of mutual trust and confidence and this caused financial loss, that loss may be recoverable in an action for wrongful dismissal (*cf. Addis* above). Although the House of Lords implied that this apparent extension to *Addis* was confined to the facts of the *BCCI* case, it may well prove useful precedent in future cases; although on a slightly different issue the House of Lords in *Johnson v Unisys Ltd* [2001] I.R.L.R. 279 refused to extend the remedies available in the common law where statute already provided a remedy by way of compensation for unfair dismissal.

The Effect of the Repudiatory Breach

It is sometimes necessary to decide whether the terms of the employment contract can exist once the repudiatory breach—the wrongful dismissal—has taken place; in other words, does the breach itself bring the contract to an end (the automatic or unilateral theory), or is it necessary for the innocent party, the employee, to accept the breach to make it effective and end the contractual relationship (the elective or bilateral theory). Common sense might suggest that the employment relationship is at

an end and thus the contract is terminated once the dismissal
has taken place; but the general law of contract makes it clear
that the breach will only become effective on the contract once it
has been accepted by the innocent party. Much of the case law
relevant to this issue has concerned instances where the
employee has sought to restrain the employer from terminating
the contract until a contractually agreed disciplinary procedure
has taken place. Consequently it is perhaps not surprising that
the courts have inclined towards the elective or bilateral theory
in order to keep the contract alive whilst correct procedures are
followed by both parties (*Gunton v Richmond upon Thames LBC*
[1980] I.C.R. 755, *Thomas Marshall (Exports) Ltd v Guinle* [1979]
Ch. 227, etc.). However, it must surely also be true that the
employment relationship is of a purely personal nature, and as
such the contract cannot continue to exist once the relationship
has been effectively terminated by a repudiatory breach.
Authority to support this automatic or unilateral theory may be
found in *Sanders v Ernest A Neale Ltd* [1974] I.R.L.R. 236 and as
obiter dicta in *Boyo v Lambeth LBC* [1995] I.R.L.R. 50.

A method of viewing this problem which has the effect of
reconciling at least some of the otherwise conflicting case law is
to consider that in contract law an innocent party may only
refuse to accept a repudiatory contract breach if they have a
"legitimate interest" in maintaining the contract. Thus, maintaining the contract during disciplinary procedure may well be a
"legitimate interest"; wishing to continue to draw wages whilst
not having to work, may not be.

The court in *Irani v Southampton and South West Hampshire HA*
[1985] I.C.R. 590 chose not to address this issue, but granted an
injunction preventing a dismissal in order to allow time for a
disciplinary procedure to take place, in circumstances where it
was held that mutual trust and confidence between the parties
still existed.

CASE EXAMPLE

Addis v Gramophone Co Ltd **[1909] A.C. 488**
Mr Addis's contract provided that he would be paid part salary
and part commission, and in the event of termination would be
entitled to six months' notice. His contract was terminated by
his employers and he was given six months' notice, but was not

allowed to work out his notice period. The question arose as to the damages to which Mr Addis was entitled.

Held: The House of Lords held that he was entitled only to the wages for the six month notice period, plus the commission he would have earned had he been permitted to work for those six months.

He was not entitled to damages as compensation for injured feelings, nor for "the loss he may sustain from the fact that his having been dismissed of itself makes it more difficult for him to obtain fresh employment."—per Lord Loreburn L.C.

Commentary: Thus compensation for wrongful dismissal amounts only to monies to which the employee would have been entitled under the contract. It will not include any discretionary bonuses or pay rises.

CASE EXAMPLE

Malik v BCCI SA [1997] I.R.L.R. 462

Mr Malik was dismissed through redundancy, following the collapse of the bank through "dishonest and corrupt business" practices. Mr Malik claimed damages for the disadvantage his association with the bank would place him under in trying to obtain further employment. It was argued that following *Addis* such damages were not available.

Held: The House of Lords held that *Addis* did not preclude the award of damages in a situation such as this, since the damages in *Malik* were in respect of the employer's breach of the contract term of mutual trust and confidence. At the time of *Addis* this contract term had not been recognised, whereas today it is implied into every employment contract; accordingly damages should be assessed for the breach of the term in line with accepted contract principles.

Commentary: On the particular facts of this case, the decision would appear to be both sensible and fair, and reflect current business realities. Although the court suggested that the decision would have little effect beyond the specifics of this case, it is very likely that future plaintiffs would wish to rely on it.

Public Law Remedies

Certain public employees may be entitled to public law remedies against their employer, by way of judicial review. This may result in an order of certiorari, quashing the decision of the employer, or *mandamus*, an order requiring an employer to perform a duty.

The circumstances in which public employees may rely on public law are very limited. In *R. v East Berkshire Area HA, Ex p. Walsh* [1984] I.C.R. 743 the Court of Appeal held that judicial review would only be available where either the matter concerned public rather than private law or where the employment relationship is not defined in contractual terms (see *Ridge v Baldwin* [1964] A.C. 40); thus most public employees would need to rely on private law for an action regarding breach of the employment contract.

---

11. UNFAIR DISMISSAL

Unfair dismissal is a statutory concept consolidated almost wholly within the ERA 1996. Section 94(1) of the ERA 1996 states:

> **"An employee has the right not to be unfairly dismissed by his employer."**

Different writers and commentators have used various formats in order to explain and try to simplify the issue of unfair dismissal. Unfair dismissal is a very broad topic and one which is almost guaranteed to appear in any employment law examination in one guise or another. It overlaps into several other areas, and can appear a daunting subject to many students. However, approached properly it is one of the most straightforward topics in employment law.

An examination question on unfair dismissal may be successfully attempted by logically working through the following four steps in order—this will both give a structure to the answer and ensure that all aspects of the question are considered:

(a) Can the applicant claim?
(b) Can a dismissal be identified?
(c) The reason for the dismissal.
(d) The fairness of the dismissal.

It is of course necessary to consider each question in detail:

CAN THE APPLICANT CLAIM?

(a) Is the applicant an employee?

It is necessary that the applicant prove their employee status as considered in Chapter 3 in order to qualify for unfair dismissal rights. However, be aware that under the ERelA 1999 powers have been granted to the relevant minister to extend existing employment rights to categories of workers not presently covered.

(b) Does the employee belong to an excluded group?

Certain categories of employees automatically fall outside the protection of the Act, these include:

(i) those over normal retirement age (s.109(1) of the ERA 1996)—this is generally held to be 65 years of age, but case law suggests that in certain circumstances a contractual term specifying a lower age may be accepted (*Brooks v British Telecom Plc* [1992] I.C.R. 414);

(ii) the armed forces (although provisions are in place to change this), the police, and in certain circumstances crown servants; and

(iii) those protected by collective agreements regulating dismissal procedures *may* be exempted—such procedures must be approved by the Secretary for State as operating as a substitute for the statutory scheme (s.110 of the ERA 1996). At present no such schemes are in operation.

(c) Does the employee have the minimum required length of continuous service?

Following the Unfair Dismissal and Statement of Reasons for Dismissal (Variation of Qualifying Period) Order 1999 (SI 1999/1436), the minimum period of continuous employment required in order to claim for unfair dismissal is one year.

In some circumstances it will be necessary to consider what is meant by the term "continuous employment". **Continuity of Employment** may be considered under two sub-headings: continuity within the contract of employment, and continuity outside the contract.

CONTINUITY WITHIN THE CONTRACT. Weeks which count towards continuity are "any week during the whole or part of which the employee's relations with the employer are governed by a contract of employment" (s.212(1) of the ERA 1996). Thus continuity may be maintained should the terms of the contract change, the place of work or job function change, and even across a series of consecutive contracts with the same employer. Any term of the contract purporting to waive continuity rights would be void under s.203 of the ERA 1996.

CONTINUITY OUTSIDE THE CONTRACT. Statute protects continuity in certain circumstances where no contract of employment is in force; these are for up to 26 weeks of sickness or injury, due to a temporary cessation of work, or in circumstances whereby through custom or arrangement such absences are not regarded as breaking continuity (s.212(3) of the ERA 1996). Examples of such situations include:

(i) Continuity was preserved for a lecturer working under a series of contracts each year from September to July, even though for the months between there was no contract subsisting. The House of Lords held that the summer months constituted a "temporary cessation of work" (*Ford v Warwickshire CC* [1983] I.R.L.R. 126).

(ii) Workers laid off and taken back on again, possibly on a number of occasions over several years, due to seasonal demand may also have continuity of employment (*Flack v Kodak Ltd* [1986] I.C.R. 775).

(iii) In deciding whether gaps in employment are sufficient to break continuity, the court in *Ford* adopted a mathematical approach by comparing the period of the break with the periods of work on either side of it, to determine whether it was "temporary". The court in *Flack*, however, used a broad brush approach to determine overall whether continuity had been preserved, rather than to examine each instance of cessation of work in its own right. Although these two methods of approach appear to be in conflict, the EAT in the case of *Sillars v Charrington Fuels Ltd* [1988] I.C.R. 505 suggested that the mathematical approach should be used when gaps are regular, but the broad brush approach is appropriate when gaps were irregular.

(iv) The EAT has recently cast some doubt on the issue of preserving continuity of employment with the decision in *Booth v United States of America* [1999] I.R.L.R. 16, in which it was stated:

> ". . . whilst it is generally desirable that employees should enjoy statutory protection during their employment, Parliament has laid down the conditions under which that protection is afforded. If, by so arranging their affairs, an employer is lawfully able to employ people in such a manner that the employees cannot complain of unfair dismissal or seek a redundancy payment, that is a matter for him. The courts simply try and apply the law as it stands."

This decision may weaken the line of authority from *Flack*, *Ford* and *Sillars*, etc.

(v) Weeks lost through industrial action will neither count towards nor break continuity of employment (s.216 of the ERA 1996).

In some situations another factor which may affect the qualifying period of service is the question of the effective date of termination of the contract. **The effective date of termination** (EDT) is defined in s.97 of the ERA 1996 as:

> "(a) where notice is given, the date on which that notice expires, (b) where no notice is given, the date on which the termination takes place, or (c) in the event of a fixed term contract not being renewed, the date on which the contract expires."

Some confusion has arisen in determining the EDT in cases of termination with money in lieu of notice. The traditional approach in *Dedman v British Building and Engineering Appliances Ltd* [1974] I.C.R. 53 was to treat money in lieu of notice as a summary dismissal and hold that the EDT was on the date the termination takes place, *i.e.* the final day of employment. However, the case of *Adams v GKN Sankey Ltd* [1980] I.R.L.R. 416 suggested that the EDT should depend upon the true construction placed on the dismissal; if the dismissal was expressed as summary dismissal, but with monies in respect of possible damages for wrongful dismissal, then the EDT should be the date of termination; if, on the other hand, the dismissal was with notice, but monies representing wages in lieu of notice were given, then the EDT should be the date on which the notice would expire. Although there is no binding authority on the point, *Adams* is to be preferred.

In cases where the contract is terminated by the employer and the minimum notice periods provided for by s.86 of the ERA 1996 would, if given, expire on a later date than the EDT, statute (s.97(2) of the ERA 1996) will intervene to hold that the later date is the EDT for the purpose of calculating the qualifying period of employment under s.108 of the ERA 1996.

(d) Has the claim been brought within time?

Section 111 of the ERA 1996 states that claims of unfair dismissal must be brought before the tribunal within three months of the EDT, although s.111(2)(b) of the ERA 1996 allows such further time as the tribunal considers reasonable if it considers that it was not reasonably practicable for the applicant to bring the case earlier. The courts have tended to interpret s.111(2)(b) of the ERA 1996 strictly:

(i) Ignorance of one's rights will not normally be sufficient (*Dedman v British Building and Engineering Appliances* [1974] I.C.R. 53).

(ii) Incorrect advice from a skilled advisor may not be sufficient (*Riley v Tesco Stores Ltd* [1980] I.C.R. 323).

(iii) Waiting for the outcome of a relevant event, *e.g.* a criminal trial, may not be sufficient (*Norgett v Luton Industrial Co-op Soc Ltd* [1976] I.C.R. 442).

(iv) Waiting for the outcome of an internal appeal system undertaken following termination may not be sufficient (*Palmer v Southend-on-Sea BC* [1984] I.C.R. 372). In such circumstances the applicant should either enter an application to the tribunal immediately following termination, or should advise the tribunal office that an investigation is being undertaken.

CAN A DISMISSAL BE IDENTIFIED?

In many situations there will be no problem in identifying the dismissal, *e.g.* "You are fired", "I'm afraid I must give you a month's notice", etc. However, in some cases the situation is much less clear.

Words and Actions

(a) If the words are clear and unambiguous the tribunal should treat them as such (*Sothern v Franks Charlesly & Co* [1981] I.R.L.R. 278).

(b) If the words are ambiguous, if they have been said in the heat of the moment, or as part of an argument or row, the tribunal may look behind the actual words used to ensure that what has taken place really is a dismissal (*Chesham Shipping Ltd v Rowe* [1977] I.R.L.R. 391).

(c) Language which may constitute a dismissal in one industry or situation, may not have the same meaning in another (*Futty v D and D Brekkes Ltd* [1974] I.R.L.R. 130).

(d) It may often be possible for words said in the heat of the moment to be withdrawn (*Martin v Yeoman Aggregates Ltd* [1983] I.R.L.R. 49), but in some cases the mere saying of the words may destroy the contractual term of mutual trust and confidence.

(e) An employee prompted to resign by the threat of dismissal, may be held to have been dismissed (*East Sussex CC v Walker* (1972) 7 I.T.R. 280).

(f) However, if the resignation is prompted not by threat of dismissal, but by the offer of a severance package, there will not be a dismissal (*Birch v University of Liverpool* [1985] I.C.R. 470).

Resignation whilst under Notice of Dismissal

If an employee is under notice of dismissal, but then gives notice of resignation to take effect before the dismissal, statute provides that for the purposes of any unfair dismissal claim the employee shall be taken to have been dismissed (s.95(2) of the ERA 1996).

Dismissal whilst Continuing in Employment

Under normal circumstances, once a dismissal takes place the employment relationship will end. However, this is not always the case. In the case of *Hogg v Dover College* [1990] I.C.R. 39, Mr Hogg, a full-time teacher, suffered an illness and was subsequently offered part-time work at a reduced salary. He worked part-time under protest but also lodged a complaint of unfair dismissal. The EAT held that he had been dismissed from his full-time position and that his part-time work was being performed under a new contract.

It is unclear how widely this approach may be used by employees to fight unilaterally imposed changes to the contract of employment; by arguing that the change imposed by the employer has caused a dismissal under the original contract, and that by continuing to work under the new terms, the employee is in fact working under a new contract. Thus, a claim for unfair dismissal could proceed, even though the employee continues in employment (see *Alcan Extrusions v Yates* [1996] I.R.L.R. 327).

Expiry of Fixed Term Contract

If the employee is employed under a fixed term contract and that contract expires without being renewed, statute deems that the employee has been dismissed (s.95(1)(b) of the ERA 1996).

A fixed term contract is one for which the date of termination of the contract is predetermined.

A fixed task contract—one that will end on the completion of a particular task or agreed amount of work—is not a fixed term contract, unless an actual date of termination is known in advance, *e.g. Wiltshire CC v NATFHE* [1980] I.C.R. 455).

Likewise, a contract which is determinable upon the happening of a future contingent event, *e.g.* a contract which it has been agreed will terminate if a particular funding source should cease, is not a fixed term contract and termination of the contract will not amount to a dismissal (*Brown v Knowsley BC* [1986] I.R.L.R. 102). Unsurprisingly, such contracts have found limited favour with the courts. Only if the contingent event is outside the control of the parties to the contract are the courts likely to accept that the contract should be treated as one "determinable on the happening of a future contingent event".

Thus the termination of either a fixed task contract or a contract determinable upon the happening of a contingent event will not give rise to a dismissal for the purpose of unfair dismissal legislation, although presumably if such contracts were terminated with or without notice before the otherwise intended end of the contract, then a dismissal would take place.

The fact that a fixed term contract may include provision for the contract to be terminated by notice by either party prior to the expiry of the fixed term does not preclude the contract from being a fixed term contract (*Dixon v BBC* [1979] Q.B. 546). Following the introduction of the ERelA 1999 it is no longer possible for employees working on fixed term contracts to waive their rights to claim unfair dismissal, although clauses in fixed term contracts waiving rights to redundancy payments continue to be lawful.

Self Dismissal

Under the general principle of contract law, if the employee commits a repudiatory breach of contract, that breach will only be effective on the contract once it has been accepted by the innocent party, the employer. Thus, it is the action of the employer which terminates the contract, and thus there is a dismissal (*London Transport Executive v Clarke* [1981] I.C.R. 355). This is not, of course, to suggest that the dismissal is unfair; indeed if the employee has committed a repudiatory breach the dismissal is likely *prima facie* to be fair.

In the case of *Igbo v Johnson Matthey Chemicals Ltd* [1986] I.R.L.R. 215, Mrs Igbo was permitted to take extended holiday on condition that she signed an agreement that should she not return to work on the agreed day her employment would automatically terminate. When she returned from holiday she was ill, so instead of returning to work she sent in a medical certificate. Her employers invoked the agreement and declared her employment terminated. The Court of Appeal, however, held that the automatic termination agreement was invalid as being contrary to s.203(1) of the ERA 1996 which makes void any term of the contract which seeks to exclude or limit any provision of the ERA; thus a dismissal had taken place.

Frustration

Any contract which is terminated by frustration does not give rise to a dismissal (*Egg Stores (Stamford Hill) Ltd v Leibovici* [1977] I.C.R. 260).

Mutual Consent

Due to the perceived inequality of bargaining powers in the employment relationship, and to the operation of s.203 of the

ERA 1996, termination by mutual consent not resulting in a dismissal will always be difficult to establish particularly in a statutory context. Cases in which the courts have found termination by mutual consent include: *SW Strange Ltd v Mann* [1965] 1 All E.R. 1069, *Lipton Ltd v Marlborough* [1979] I.R.L.R. 179, both concerning restraint clauses, *Birch v University of Liverpool* [1985] I.C.R. 470 and *Scott v Coalite Fuels Ltd* [1988] I.C.R. 355 both concerning voluntary early retirement schemes—it should be stressed though that these cases are very much the exception to the rule, and mutual consent is rarely established.

Constructive Dismissal

> "... an employee is dismissed by his employer if ... the employee terminates the contract under which he is employed (with or without notice) in circumstances in which he is entitled to terminate it without notice by reason of the employer's conduct" (s.95(1)(c) of the ERA 1996).

The question to be asked is, do the actions of the employer constitute a fundamental breach of a term of the contract? If they do, then the employee can claim constructive dismissal.

The leading case, *Western Excavating (ECC) Ltd v Sharp* [1978] Q.B. 761, confirms that the correct test to be applied to determine whether the actions of the employer permit the employee to terminate the contract and claim constructive dismissal is a "contractual test" not a "reasonableness test". In other words, is the action taken by the employer in accordance with the terms of the contract? Rather than "has the employer acted reasonably?"

Constructive dismissal may therefore be said to be where the employee terminates the contract due to the employer either committing a fundamental breach of the contract, or evincing clear intentions not to be bound by it.

Although this appears quite straightforward, case law has resulted in some decisions which on the face of it do not appear consistent, and the following principles may be helpful:

(a) an employer cannot be in breach of a contract term by invoking that term, however unreasonable his actions may be (*Western Excavating v Sharp*); but,

(b) by invoking a contract term in an unreasonable manner an employer may be in breach of the fundamental term of "mutual trust and confidence" (*United Bank Ltd v Akhtar* [1989] I.R.L.R. 507).

The duty of mutual trust and confidence has over the years grown in both scope and importance, and for the purposes of constructive dismissal, has included:

(a) use of abusive language by the employer (*Isle of Wight Tourist Board v Coombes* [1976] I.R.L.R. 413);
(b) failure to allow an employee reasonable access to a grievance procedure (*WA Goold (Pearmak) Ltd v McConnell* [1995] I.R.L.R. 516);
(c) refusing to investigate a health and safety complaint (*British Aircraft Corp v Austin* [1978] I.R.L.R. 332;
(d) failure to take seriously a complaint of sexual harassment (*Bracebridge Engineering Ltd v Darby* [1990] I.R.L.R. 3);
(e) "arbitrarily" and "capriciously" refusing an employee a pay rise (*FC Gardiner v Beresford* [1978] I.R.L.R. 63);
(f) insisting on relocating an employee in the absence of any contractual mobility clause (*Aparau v Iceland Frozen Foods Ltd* [1996] I.R.L.R. 119);
(g) disproportionate punishment of an employee for a minor offence (*BBC v Beckett* [1983] I.R.L.R. 43); and
(h) allowing an employee to be sexually harassed (*Western Excavating*, and see also *Burton v De Vere Hotels*).

Although constructive dismissal is usually brought about by a single serious act of the employer, a series of minor incidents may be sufficient (*Woods v WM Car Services (Peterborough) Ltd* [1981] I.C.R. 666).

Finally, remember that a constructive dismissal is not the same as an unfair dismissal. Usually a finding of constructive dismissal will also lead to the finding of an unfair dismissal, but on occasions the courts have found a constructive dismissal to be fair (*Savoia v Chiltern Herb Farms Ltd* [1981] I.R.L.R. 65).

THE REASON FOR THE DISMISSAL

Statute identifies only five potentially fair reasons for dismissal (s.98(1)(b) of the ERA 1996), and to successfully defend a claim of unfair dismissal an employer must initially establish that the reason for dismissal falls within one or more of these categories.

The potentially fair reasons are:

(a) capability or qualifications;
(b) conduct;
(c) redundancy;
(d) contravention of a statute; and
(e) some other substantial reason.

Capability or Qualifications

This category may include such issues as skill, aptitude, general ability or ill-health. If the issue is one of incompetence, even one instance may constitute sufficient grounds (*Taylor v Alidair Ltd* [1978] I.R.L.R. 82).

CASE EXAMPLE

International Sports Co Ltd v Thompson **[1980] I.R.L.R. 340**
In the last 18 months of employment with International Sports, Ms Thompson was off sick for a total of some five months. Her medical certificates ranged from dizzy spells, to viral infections and flatulence. In agreement with the trade union the company issued a series of warnings to her and reviewed her medical history which consisted of a series of unrelated, transitory complaints, and finally dismissed her for unsatisfactory performance. She then claimed unfair dismissal.

Held: The dismissal was fair. The company had carried out reasonable investigation into her absences, given her the opportunity to respond, issued warnings and in the absence of any improvement in her attendance, were justified in dismissing her.

Commentary: Much of the previous case law concerned employees dismissed for absence due to serious and prolonged illness, *e.g. East Lindsey DC v Daubney* [1977] I.R.L.R. 181. Although this case was considered on the grounds of conduct, in cases such as this, dismissal will normally be on the grounds of capability since the company would probably not wish to prove that the employee was actually malingering.

Conduct

Conduct has been held to include dishonesty (*British Home Stores v Burchell* [1978] I.R.L.R. 379), fighting at work (*Meakin v Liverpool CC* (EAT/142/00), refusal to obey instructions (*Atkin v Enfield Hospital* [1975] I.R.L.R. 217), breach of health and safety regulations (*Wilcox v Humphries & Glasgow Ltd* [1975] I.R.L.R. 211, etc.

Redundancy

Dismissal on the grounds of redundancy is a potentially fair reason for dismissal. This issue is dealt with more fully in Chapter 12.

Contravention of a Statute

This category would include both the situation in which the circumstance of the employee changes so that his continued employment would become unlawful, *e.g.* a driver who is subsequently banned by the courts from driving and also the rare situation where the law changes, making it unlawful to continue to employ someone in a particular job.

Some Other Substantial Reason (SOSR)

This category has been variously termed a "catch-all" or "dust-bin" category. It is broad, including such issues as:

(a) Failure by an employee to adapt (*Cresswell v Board of Inland Revenue* [1984] I.C.R. 508).
(b) Clash of personalities (*Treganowan v Robert Knee & Co Ltd* [1975] I.C.R. 405).
(c) Mistaken belief that employee did not have work permit (*Bouchaala v THF Hotels Ltd* [1980] I.C.R. 721).
(d) Failure by employee to disclose medical history when asked at interview (*O'Brien v Prudential Assurance Co Ltd* [1979] I.R.L.R. 140).
(e) Refusal of an employee to accept a new contract term which the employer held "necessary" (*RS Components v Irwin* [1973] I.C.R. 535).
(f) Pressure from a third party (*Saunders v Scottish National Camps Association* [1980] I.R.L.R. 174).

(g) Refusal of an employee to accept a drop in wages from £130 to £90 per week negotiated with the trade union (*Sycamore v H Myer & Co Ltd* [1976] I.R.L.R. 84).

The list is by no means exclusive.

Automatically Unfair Reasons

Certain reasons for dismissal (or for selection for redundancy) are automatically unfair.

Assertion of statutory right (s.104 of the ERA 1996). Section 104 of the ERA 1996 makes a dismissal automatically unfair if the reason, or principle reason, for it is that the employee had brought proceedings against the employer to enforce a "relevant statutory right". Such rights are any of the rights contained in ERA for which the remedy is via a complaint to an employment tribunal, the right to a minimum notice period, and rights relating to deductions from pay, trade union activities and time off contained in the TULR(C)A 1992. There is no minimum qualifying period necessary to bring a claim.

Pregnancy and maternity (s.99 of the ERA 1996). Dismissal of a worker on the grounds of pregnancy is automatically unfair; there is no qualifying period necessary to bring a claim; and probably no defence available to the employer (but see *Webb v EMO Air Cargo (UK) Ltd* [1995] I.R.L.R. 645).

Trade union membership or non-membership (s.137 of the TULR(C)A 1992). It is automatically unfair to dismiss a worker for joining, being a member of, refusing to join or refusing to remain a member of a trade union. There is no minimum qualifying period necessary to bring such a claim.

Dismissal of striking employees (ERelA 1999). The dismissal of an employee for taking part in official industrial action is automatically unfair if it occurs within the first eight weeks of such participation. A dismissal after that period may also be unfair if the employer fails to take reasonable steps to resolve the dispute.

Employee representatives (s.103 of the ERA 1996). Dismissal of an employees' representative (under Ch II, Pt IV of the

TULR(C)A 1992) or a candidate for election to such a position is automatically unfair if the principle reason for such a dismissal relates to the activities of the role.

Health and safety (s.100 of the ERA 1996). Particular protection is afforded by s.100 of the ERA 1996 to health and safety representatives and members of health and safety committees, and also to workers in companies in which there is no health and safety representative or committee, to make automatically unfair any dismissal on the grounds that the employee was carrying out health and safety duties. No qualifying period is necessary to bring such a claim.

Sunday work (s.101 of the ERA 1996). Certain groups of shop workers are protected against dismissal for refusal to work on Sundays (Pt IV of the ERA 1996).

Transfer of undertakings (TUPE 1981). Dismissal in connection with a transfer of undertakings falling within the 1981 Regulations is automatically unfair, although there are "economic, technical or organisational" defences open to an employer. A one-year qualifying period is necessary for employees in this category.

Trustees of occupational pension schemes (s.102 of the ERA 1996). Protected if the reason or principle reason for the dismissal is that the employee performed any function as such a trustee.

THE FAIRNESS OF THE DISMISSAL

Once it has been shown that the applicant is qualified to make a claim, that a dismissal has taken place, and that the employer has put forward a potentially fair reason for the dismissal, only then is it necessary to consider the fairness of the dismissal.

Section 98(4) of the ERA 1996 states that:

> "the determination of the question whether the dismissal is fair or unfair (having regard to the reason shown by the employer) depends on whether in the circumstances (including the size and administrative resources of the employer's undertaking) the employer acted reasonably or unreasonably in treating it as a sufficient reason for dismissing the employee, and shall be determined in accordance with equity and the substantial merits of the case."

The fairness of the dismissal may be divided into two broad headings, both of which must be satisfied in order to prove a fair dismissal: the **band of reasonable responses**, and **procedural fairness**.

Band of Reasonable Responses

> "[The] tribunal must consider the reasonableness of the employer's conduct, not simply whether they [the members of the industrial tribunal] consider the dismissal to be fair; in judging the reasonableness of the employer's conduct an industrial tribunal must not substitute its decision as to what was the right course to adopt for that of the employer; in many, though not all, cases there is a band of reasonable responses to the employee's conduct within which one employer might reasonably take one view, another quite reasonably take another; the function of the industrial tribunal . . . is to determine whether in the particular circumstances of each case the decision to dismiss the employee fell within the band of reasonable responses which a reasonable employer might have adopted." (*Iceland Frozen Foods v Jones* [1983] I.C.R. 17, per Browne-Wilkinson J.).

Thus in summary, the tribunal must not ask, "What would we have done in that situation?" But instead, in effect, "Could a reasonable employer have done what was done?" If so, at this stage, the dismissal will be fair.

Obviously, the range of reasonable responses may be very broad, and have included:

(a) The dismissal of an attendant at a boys' camp solely on the grounds of his homosexuality (*Saunders v Scottish National Camps Association* [1980] I.R.L.R. 174).

(b) The dismissal of a rail steward of 14 years' service for having in his possession food, in contravention of a regulation prohibiting employees engaging in business on their own account (*British Railways Board v Jackson* [1994] I.R.L.R. 235).

(c) The dismissal of both employees where it was believed that one was guilty of theft, but it could not be ascertained which (*Monie v Coral Racing Ltd* [1981] I.C.R. 109).

Thus, the range of reasonable responses to a situation of, *e.g.* horseplay at work could range from an informal rebuke, a formal warning, to dismissal. Each of these responses may be considered fair.

Doubt was cast on the band of reasonable responses test by the EAT in the case of *Haddon v Van Den Bergh Foods Ltd* [1999] I.R.L.R. 672, who considered that because of the ease with which the test may be satisfied by an employer, the test was "a test of perversity". These views were, however firmly overruled by the Court of Appeal in the joined cases of *Post Office v Foley; HSBC (formerly Midland Bank) v Madden* [2000] I.R.L.R. 827 who confirmed that the band of reasonable responses test should continue to be applied in accordance with binding case law.

Procedural Fairness

It has been possible for a dismissal for a fair reason, which is within the range of reasonable responses, to be found unfair if it failed the test of procedural fairness.

ACAS have a Code of Practice which, whilst not having the force of law, may be relied upon as a blueprint for an employer's own disciplinary code; the Code lays down a system of warnings for misconduct, etc. and follows the principles of natural justice. If an employer abides by the ACAS Code it is most unlikely if not almost impossible that a tribunal would hold that a dismissal was procedurally unfair.

The House of Lords in the case of *Polkey v AE Dayton Services Ltd* [1988] I.C.R. 142, stressed the importance of following an agreed procedure in disciplinary hearings, holding that a failure to follow such procedure was likely to result in a finding of unfair dismissal, unless "the employer could reasonably have concluded in the light of circumstances known at the time of dismissal that consultation or warning would be utterly useless".

Due to come into effect from Summer/Autumn 2003, a major change to the issue of procedural fairness has been introduced by the EA 2002 which has amended s.98 of the ERA 1996 by the introduction of s.98A of the ERA 1996:

> "(2) Subject to subsection (1), an employee who is dismissed shall not be regarded for the purposes of this Part as unfairly dismissed because of failure by the employer to follow a procedure in relation to the dismissal if the employer shows that he would have decided to dismiss the employee if he had followed the procedure."

It therefore seems that the fundamental question for the tribunal will be whether the relevant statutory procedure has been followed, rather than whether a procedurally fair process has been followed (*cf. Polkey*).

This **statutory dispute resolution procedure** is set out in Sch 2 to the Act and consists of three steps:

Step 1—The employer must set out in writing the issues which have caused the employer to contemplate taking action and send a copy of this statement to the employee inviting him to attend a meeting.

Step 2—The meeting should take place before action is taken and the employee should take all steps to attend. After the meeting the employer should inform the employee of the decision and notify him of his right of appeal.

Step 3—If the employee wishes to appeal, a further meeting should be arranged at which the parties should attend and after which the employee should be notified of the outcome. The dismissal or other disciplinary action decided upon in step 2 may be instigated prior to the second (*i.e.* appeal) meeting taking place.

It therefore appears that as long as this statutory procedure has been followed, other issues of procedural fairness may no longer be relevant—the fairness of the dismissal turning wholly on issues of substantive fairness. It remains to be seen what effect such issues as denial of natural justice may have in this area of law.

Generally in assessing the fairness of a dismissal the tribunal may only take into account facts known to the employer at the time of dismissal (*W Devis & Sons Ltd v Atkins* [1977] A.C. 931), but the House of Lords in *West Midlands Co-operative Society Ltd v Tipton* [1986] A.C. 536 held that facts arising out of a post-dismissal appeal may also be taken into account by the tribunal. The effect of this is that if an employee is denied an appeal to which he is contractually entitled, the dismissal will almost certainly be unfair.

A drawing together of many of the principles of unfair dismissal may be seen from the case of *British Home Stores v Burchell* [1978] I.R.L.R. 379 in which the employee was dismissed because the employer believed she was stealing on a staff discount scheme.

Ms Burchell fulfilled the requirements necessary for her to make a claim.

The reason put forward for her dismissal was conduct—her alleged theft. The EAT laid down a three part test:

(a) that the employer honestly held the belief;
(b) that the employer had reasonable grounds on which to sustain that belief; and
(c) that the employer had carried out as much investigation as was reasonable in all the circumstances.

It is important to note that the question for the tribunal did not concern the guilt or innocence of Ms Burchell, but the question of whether in view of the facts as they were known to the employer at the time, the employer acted reasonably both in the decision and the manner of her dismissal.

For a further consideration of the *Burchell* test see the recent case of *Boys and Girls Welfare Society v McDonald* [1996] I.R.L.R. 129, but bear in mind that following the implementation of the EA 2002, the courts would now need to consider whether the parties had followed the statutory dispute resolution procedure.

Remedies for Unfair Dismissal

The tribunal may award any of three remedies as may be requested by the successful applicant: reinstatement, re-engagement, or compensation.

REINSTATEMENT requires the employer to treat the employee as if he had not been dismissed, making good arrears of pay, any increments or improvements in terms and conditions to which the employee would have been entitled, etc.

RE-ENGAGEMENT requires the employer to engage the employee on the same or comparable work, on terms and conditions such as the tribunal may require, including such matters as an amount for pay arrears, etc.

The main problem with orders for both reinstatement and re-engagement is that in most cases by this stage the duty of mutual trust and confidence between the employer and the employee will have broken down, making such orders unworkable.

COMPENSATION may take the form of a basic award computed in the same way as a redundancy payment, a compensatory award to reflect the loss sustained by the applicant due to the dismissal, an additional award should the employer not comply with a reinstatement or re-engagement order and a special award payable only in cases of trade union membership or health and safety dismissals.

---

12. REDUNDANCY

". . . a worker of long standing is now recognised as having an accrued right in his job; and his right gains in value with the years. So much so that if the job is shut down he is entitled to compensation for loss of the job . . . The worker gets a redundancy payment. It is not unemployment pay . . . Even if he gets another job straightaway, he nevertheless is entitled to full redundancy payment. It is, in a real sense, compensation for long service. No man gets it unless he has been employed for at least two years by the employer; and then the amount of it depends solely upon his age and length of service." *Lloyd v Brassey* [1969] 2 Q.B. 98, per Lord Denning M.R.

Section 139(1) of the ERA states:

> "For the purposes of this Act an employee who is dismissed shall be taken to be dismissed by reason of redundancy if the dismissal is wholly or mainly attributable to —
>
> (a) the fact that his employer has ceased or intends to cease—
>   (i) to carry on the business for the purposes of which the employee was employed by him, or
>   (ii) to carry on that business in the place where the employee was so employed,
>   or
> (b) the fact that the requirements of that business—
>   (i) for employees to carry out work of a particular kind, or
>   (ii) for employees to carry out work of a particular kind in the place where the employee was employed by the employer,
>   have ceased or diminished or are expected to cease or diminish."

Although at first glance this appears fairly straightforward, there are in particular two areas of concern: what is meant by "work of a particular kind" and what is the "place of work"?

Work of a particular kind

CONTRACT TEST V JOB FUNCTION TEST V STATUTORY TEST

Different approaches have been adopted by the courts in the past. The earlier "job function test" called on the court to consider whether the overall function of the role, rather than the specific work detailed in the employment contract, had changed. If the function had remained then any dismissal would not have been on the grounds of redundancy.

An example of this can be seen in the case of *North Riding Garages v Butterwick* [1967] 2 Q.B. 56, in which an employee of 30 years' service had worked his way up to workshop manager although he still spent much of his time working as a hands-on mechanic. New owners took over and required the workshop manager to concentrate more of his time on sales and paper-work, which he was unable to do satisfactorily. After some months he was dismissed, and he claimed redundancy. In holding that he was not redundant, the court stated that employees have a duty to adapt to new methods and tech-niques, and only if the new methods alter the nature of the work required may they be redundant. In the case of Mr Butterwick his function as workshop manager remained, thus he was not redundant.

The later "contract test" required the court to consider the range of work the employee could be called upon to perform under their contract—rather than merely the actual work the employee has been doing—and if this work had diminished or ceased the employee would be redundant. This may be illus-trated by the case of *Nelson v BBC* [1980] I.C.R. 100, in which the employee was employed as a producer and editor for the BBC. He had worked for much of his career in the Caribbean Service, and when this service was closed down the question arose as to whether Mr Nelson was redundant. The Court of Appeal held that although there was a diminution in the specific work Mr Nelson had actually been doing, there was no such diminution in the work of producers and editors generally, which was the work he was contracted to do; thus Mr Nelson was not redundant.

A third approach—a "statutory test"—has recently been introduced by the EAT in the case of *Safeway Stores plc v Burrell* [1997] I.R.L.R. 200, as follows:

(a) Was the employee dismissed?

(b) If so, was there a diminution or cessation in the requirements of the employer's business for employees (not the
employee) to carry out work of a particular kind or an
expectation of such in the future?

(c) If so, was the dismissal of the employee caused wholly or
mainly by that state of affairs?

The terms of the employee's contract of employment are not
relevant for consideration at the second stage; they will only
become relevant, if at all, at the third stage.

Application of this "statutory test" allows for the principle of
"bumping" whereby an employee may be made redundant, not
because his own job is redundant, but because his job has been
filled by another employee who would otherwise themselves
have been made redundant.

Although this "statutory test" was itself doubted by a differently constituted EAT in the case of *Church v West Lancashire
NHS Trust* [1998] I.R.L.R. 4, which stated that the proper test is a
"sensible blend" of the contractual and functional approaches,
the House of Lords in *Murray v Foyle Meats* [1999] I.R.L.R. 562
has confirmed that the "statutory" test is to be applied and that
both the "contract" test and the "job function" test are themselves redundant and should not be followed. Their Lordships
stated that if a dismissal is attributable to a redundancy situation, the dismissal will be by way of redundancy.

This important case both clarifies and indeed simplifies the
situation and also impliedly confirms the lawfulness of bumped
redundancies.

Place of Work

The problem faced by the court has been to decide whether the
inclusion of a mobility clause in the employee's contract should
be the deciding factor in defining the place of work with
reference to redundancy.

If a purely contractual approach is taken, and if the
employee's contract contains a general mobility clause, an
employer may avoid a redundancy situation by offering the
employee work in any location—which considering the case of
Western Excavating (see "constructive dismissal") would perhaps
appear to be the correct approach.

Although in the case of *O'Brien v Associated Fire Alarms Ltd*
[1968] 1 W.L.R. 1916 the court adopted a contractual test, in the

later case of *Bass Leisure Ltd v Thomas* [1994] I.R.L.R. 104 the EAT instead applied a geographical approach, looking at where the applicant had actually worked, rather than at where he could have worked. This has been supported by the Court of Appeal decision in *High Table Ltd v Horst* [1997] I.R.L.R. 513, which favoured the factual or geographical approach to "place of work". It is presently arguable whether, following *Murray v Foyle Meats*, this is still a contentious issue.

CASE EXAMPLE

High Table Ltd v Horst **[1997] I.R.L.R. 513**
Ms Horst had worked for High Table, a catering services company, as a waitress for a number of years at the premises of one of their clients, Hill Samuel, in the City of London. Following a downturn in the business between High Table and Hill Samuel in 1993, Ms Horst was made redundant.

She argued that since her employment contract contained an express mobility clause—which purported to allow the employer to transfer staff on a temporary or permanent basis to any location—her "place of work" was at any of her employer's clients, and not just at Hill Samuels. She maintained that she could and should have been offered work elsewhere, thus was not redundant, and claimed unfair dismissal.

Held: The Court of Appeal rejected her argument, coming down in favour of a factual approach, and stating:

> "If an employee has worked in only one location under his contract of employment . . . it defies common sense to widen the extent of the place where he was so employed, merely because of the existence of a mobility clause. Of course, the refusal by the employee to obey a lawful requirement under the contract of employment to move may constitute a valid reason for dismissal, but issues of dismissal, redundancy and reasonableness in the actions of an employer should be kept distinct."—*per* Peter Gibson L.J.

Commentary: Presumably therefore, place of work is factual. Even if the employee has a mobility clause in the contract, if there is a downturn of work in one particular location in which the employer has always worked, this may constitute redundancy. On the other hand, should the employer choose instead to transfer the employee to another location, rather than declare him redundant, then following *Western Excavating*, this will be lawful; unless either the reason for the transfer or the manner of the transfer breach the implied duty of trust and confidence (*United Bank v Akhtar*), in which case it may lead to unfair dismissal.

Who is Eligible?

The claimant must firstly be an employee, they must have been dismissed (s.136 of the ERA 1996), and they must have a minimum of two years' continuous employment (s.155 of the ERA 1996; *cf.* one year requirement for unfair dismissal) on the "relevant date" (s.145 of the ERA 1996)—the relevant date being either the date on which notice expires, or in the case of termination without notice, the date on which termination takes effect. However, in certain circumstances where the minimum notice period required by s.86 of the ERA 1996 would, if given, have expired at a later date, that later date will be the relevant date (s.145(5) of the ERA 1996).

In addition, certain categories are excluded from redundancy rights including:

(a) those aged under 20 (s.211 of the ERA 1996) and those over normal retirement age (if no retirement age is specified, those over 65) (s.156 of the ERA 1996); and

(b) those dismissed for misconduct or industrial action, (s.140 of the ERA 1996).

Continuity of employment

As stated above, to be eligible for redundancy an employee must have a minimum of two years continuous employment. In certain instances continuity of employment will be preserved, even though the employee apparently changes employers:

(a) Associated Employers. The business of the employer together with the business of his associated employers will be treated as one (s.139(2) of the ERA 1996), and companies are treated as associated if either one has control of the other, or both are controlled by a third party (s.231 of the ERA 1996).

(b) Transfer of Business. If a trade, business or undertaking is transferred the period of employment at the time of the transfer counts as a period of employment with the transferee (s.218(2) of the ERA 1996).

   In the case of the sale of a business this normally means that there must be the transfer of the business as a going concern—probably including the goodwill—and not merely the sale of individual assets (*Melon v Hector Powe Ltd* [1981] I.C.R. 43).

Procedure

In order to ensure that the redundancy should not be held to amount to an unfair dismissal it is important that the employer should follow a procedure of good industrial practice, such as was laid down in the case of *Williams v Compair Maxam Ltd* [1982] I.C.R. 156:

(a) The employer should give as much warning as possible.
(b) The employer should consult with the trade union, particularly regarding selection procedure.
(c) The selection procedure should be objective.
(d) The employer should ensure that the selection procedure is followed.
(e) The employer should seek to offer alternative employment.

In relation to the guidelines from *Compair*, the following points should also be considered:

(a) In situations where there is a proposal to make more than 20 redundancies the employer has a statutory duty to consult with the union or other appropriate representatives (s.188 of the TULR(C)A 1992). Note, however, that the employer's duty is to consult, not to agree, with the union—the final decision is the employer's.
(b) There is no clear authority on how closely the tribunal may examine the procedure adopted for redundancy selection. Certainly, the more transparent the system, *e.g.* LIFO (last in first out) the more likely it is that the tribunal will not question it (*British Aerospace Plc v Green* [1995] I.C.R. 1006).
(c) Certain selections for redundancy will be automatically unfair, *e.g.* trade union activities (s.153 of the TULR(C)A 1992), pregnancy, etc.

(d) If the employer makes an offer of suitable alternative
employment to an employee before the end of his
employment, there are two possible consequences:
(i) if the employee accepts the offer, then subject to a
four week trial period, there will be no dismissal; or
(ii) if the employee unreasonably refuses the offer he
will be barred from claiming a redundancy payment.

The question then arises, what constitutes "suitable alternative employment"? In the case of *Taylor v Kent CC* [1969] 2 Q.B.
560, a head teacher whose school was merged with another was
offered a post as supply teacher, but at his old salary. The court
agreed that the demotion in status was sufficient to make the
new position unsuitable. Likewise, generally a drop in pay or
earning potential will make a new position unsuitable, but since
suitability is a question of fact for the tribunal, this need not
always be the case (see, *Sheppard v NCB* [1966] 1 K.I.R. 101).

The second issue for the tribunal is whether the refusal of the
offer is unreasonable. Here the test is subjective, and the
tribunal may take into account such personal factors as
health, family commitments, etc. (*John Fowler Ltd v Parkin* [1975]
I.R.L.R. 89).

Compensation

Redundancy compensation is calculated as follows:

(a) For each year worked over the age of 18 but under the
age of 22, half a week's gross pay.
(b) For each year worked over the age of 22 but under the
age of 41, one week's gross pay.
(c) For each year worked over the age of 41 but under
normal retirement, one and a half week's pay.
(d) A maximum of 20 years of employment can be taken into
account (s.162(3) of the ERA 1996). Also be aware of the
statutory maximum amount for the basic calculation of "a
week's pay".

13. TRANSFER OF UNDERTAKINGS

Common Law Position

Since the common law holds that the contract of employment is a personal contract and not an asset of the company as such, it follows that the sale or transfer of a business would have the effect of terminating the contract, rather than transferring it. It is uncertain what effect the common law would have on the individual contracts of employment; they may on occasion be determined automatically without breach (*Re General Rolling Stock Co* (1866) L.R. 1 Eq. 346), or they may be terminated by breach giving rise to a claim for wrongful dismissal (*Nokes v Doncaster Amalgamated Collieries Ltd* [1940] A.C. 1014). However, since the intervention of statute through redundancy, unfair dismissal and more recently regulations governing transfers of undertakings, the common law position has little relevance in practice.

Transfer of Undertakings (Protection of Employment) Regulations 1981 (TUPE)

TUPE as amended were introduced to implement EC Directive 77/187 (the Acquired Rights Directive). Although the regulations are fairly complex—and certainly much case law has been generated both by the regulations and the Directive—the main thrust of the regulations is contained in reg.5.

> 5(1) ". . . a relevant transfer shall not operate so as to terminate the contract of employment of any person employed by the transferor in the undertaking or part transferred but any such contract which would otherwise have been terminated by the transfer shall have effect after the transfer as if originally made between the person so employed and the transferee."
>
> 5(2)(a) "all the transferor's rights, powers, duties and liabilities under or in connection with any such contract, shall be transferred by virtue of this Regulation to the transferee;"

Thus the contracts of employment of all employees of the transferor are automatically transferred to the transferee on the same terms and conditions as were previously enjoyed by the employees. If an employee objects to his contract being transferred he is entitled to refuse, but the effect of this is to terminate the contract *without a dismissal taking place* (reg.5(4A)(4B)).

Only if the proposed transfer would result in a significant and detrimental change to the employee may the employee terminate the contract and claim unfair dismissal via constructive dismissal (reg.5(5)). It is not firmly established whether such a claim would lie against the transferee as well as the transferor.

"Undertaking"

TUPE defines an "undertaking" as including any trade or business, but this definition has been widened following the case of *Dr Sophie Redmond Stichting v Bartol* [1992] I.R.L.R. 366 to include non-commercial organisations, *e.g.* charities. However, "activities involving the exercise of public authority" are not included (*Henke v Gemeinde Schierke und Verwaltungsgemeinschaft Brocken* [1996] I.R.L.R. 701).

"Relevant transfer"

The ECJ in *Suzen v Zehnacker Gebaudereinigung GmbH Krankenhausservice* [1997] I.R.L.R. 255 held that the transfer must relate to "a stable economic entity whose activity is not limited to performing one specific works contract"; and by so doing apparently overruled the authority of cases such as *Schmidt v Spar-und Leihkasse usw* [1994] I.R.L.R. 302 which had held that the transfer of a single individual employee to a sub-contractor could amount to a relevant transfer. It is possible to view *Suzen* as suggesting that the courts will look to find a transfer of physical assets rather than merely a transfer of labour before holding that the transfer is a "relevant transfer" and falls within the ambit of the Directive and regulations—if so, this would certainly appear to be contrary to the purpose of the Directive.

This is not, however, to suggest that a transfer may take place merely on the sale of an undertaking's assets. The ECJ in the case of *Spijkers v Gebroeders Benedik Abattoir CV* [1986] 2 C.M.L.R. 296 stated that a transfer will only take place within the meaning of the Directive if the entity in question retains its identity, in other words if the organisation is transferred as a going concern, probably including goodwill.

Other points of note include:

(a) The Directive and the regulations apply both to the contracting-out of services and to the process of compulsory competitive tendering (CCT) (*Rask v ISS Kantineservice* [1993] I.R.L.R. 133, but consider the possible limitations imposed by *Suzen*).

(b) Neither the Directive nor the regulations consider as relevant transfers changes of ownership brought about by share purchases.

(c) Some of the post-*Suzen* case law appears confusing and contradictory. The Court of Appeal in the case of *ECM (Vehicle Delivery Service) Ltd v Cox* [1999] I.C.R. 1162 held that the economic entity which was transferred was a contract to do work and the work done under that contract, rather than any tangible assets. It may be that the court in this case was particularly influenced by the fact that the company involved specifically attempted to avoid the application of TUPE.

Dismissal of Employees

Regulation 8(1) of the TUPE 1981 provides that if an employee is dismissed either before or after a relevant transfer, and the reason or principle reason for that dismissal is the transfer, that dismissal will be regarded as unfair.

However, reg.8(2) of the TUPE 1981 then allows either the transferor or the transferee the complete defence of "some other substantial reason" for the dismissal on the grounds of "economic, technical or organisational" (ETO) reasons. This may be taken to mean that in such a situation the employee would not even be entitled to a redundancy payment, however the EAT in the case of *Gorictree v Jenkinson* [1985] I.C.R. 51 held that the reg.8 ETO defence is not synonymous with the s.98 of the ERA 1996 SOSR, and thus entitlement to a redundancy payment would not be lost.

The following points should also be noted:

(a) The transferee cannot escape liability by arranging that the transferor should dismiss surplus staff before the transfer takes place. In the case of *Litster v Forth Dry Dock and Engg Co Ltd* [1989] I.C.R. 341 the respondent company was in receivership and agreed to dismiss the workforce before the transfer took place, so as to make the transfer more attractive to the transferee by attempting to avoid for the transferee any liability under the TUPE 1981 (the transferor being in receivership and with the debtors having realised their security, there were insufficient assets to meet the transferor's liability for unfair dismissal or redundancy claims). The House of Lords adopted a purposive approach to the legislation however, and stated that reg.5(3) of the TUPE 1981 should be read as if the words "or would have been so employed if he had not been unfairly dismissed. . ." had been inserted after ". . . a person so employed immediately before the trans- fer. . ." Thus the dismissed employees were brought within the scope of the regulations, and the transferee became responsible for their dismissal.

(b) Liability for unfair dismissal may be automatically passed from the transferor to the transferee, even though the transferee may not have been party to any of the prior discussions (*Thompson v Walon Car Delivery and BRS Automotive Ltd* [1997] I.R.L.R. 343).

CASE EXAMPLE

Berriman v Delabole Slate Ltd [1985] I.R.L.R. 305

Mr Berriman's employers sold their business as a going concern to Delabole Slate, who wished to bring the terms of the new employees into line with their existing staff. This would result in a decrease in guaranteed pay for Mr Berriman, who rejected the offer, left and claimed unfair dismissal.

Held: Initially the tribunal held that the dismissal was for an "economic, technical or organisational reason" and did not therefore constitute unfair dismissal. Both the EAT and the Court of Appeal took a different view. They held that the reason for the dismissal was that the new employer wished to change employment terms and conditions of the transferred staff, and that "the reason itself does not involve any change either in the number or the functions of the workforce".

Commentary: The court appears to have adopted a purposive approach, and at first glance this decision appears to afford considerable protection to transferred workers. However, the question that needs to be asked is for how long could this situation continue—at what point would a change in the transferred employee's terms cease to be as a result of the transfer, and become a potentially fair SOSR?

Consultation over transfers

There is a duty under reg.10 of the TUPE 1981 to both inform and consult with employees' representatives prior to any relevant transfer. The grounds for consultation include the timing of the transfer, the reasons for it and the legal, economic and social implications (reg.10(2) of the TUPE 1981).

Employee representatives may be either trade union representatives or non-union worker representatives, perhaps elected solely for the consultation process.

CASE EXAMPLE

Betts v Brintel Helicopters Ltd and KLM Era Helicopters (UK) Ltd [1997] I.R.L.R. 361
Brintel had provided helicopter services under three contracts to Shell (UK) Ltd. When the contracts expired, Brintel were re-awarded two of them, but the third was won by KLM. KLM did not take over any of Brintel's helicopters or staff, nor did they use the same flying base. Although some of Brintel's staff were re-deployed within Brintel's other operations, some, including Betts, were not. Betts claimed unfair dismissal.

The question for the court was whether there had been a transfer of undertakings between KLM and Brintel, if so, the dismissal may well have been unfair under the TUPE 1981.

Held: The Court of Appeal followed the recently decided case of *Suzen* and held that there had been no transfer. It argued that although the operation of the third contract by Brintel had amounted to an undertaking or economic entity, that undertaking had not been transferred. They reasoned that since very few of Brintel's assets had passed to KLM, there was insufficient evidence to show that the undertaking had retained its identity in the hands of KLM.

Commentary: In this case there is evidence that had Betts and others not claimed for unfair dismissal they may well have been engaged by KLM, arguably this should have strengthened the case that a transfer had taken place. However, the court needed to give full consideration to the recently given judgement of the ECJ in the case of *Suzen*. One potential effect of *Suzen* is that transfers may be more difficult to prove the more labour intensive a business becomes, since *Suzen* places considerable emphasis on the transfer of physical assets in proving a genuine transfer of an economic entity.

In this case remember that if the transfer of undertakings had been proved, the applicants' remedy would lie against both the transferor and the transferee (see also *Litster v Forth Dry Dock*).

14. RESTRAINT OF TRADE

A distinction must be drawn between competition during the employment relationship and competition once the relationship has ended.

Competition whilst employed

Competition during the life of the employment contract will usually fall foul of the implied duty of fidelity imposed on the employee, and amount to a breach of contract by the employee; it may also enable the employer to obtain an injunction against a third party, restraining them from employing the employee whilst the original contract is in force (*Hivac Ltd v Park Royal Scientific Instruments Ltd* [1946] Ch. 169).

The situation is less certain in the case of an employee who is working for an employer only on a part-time basis. Whilst in theory the employer could seek an injunction to prevent the employee working elsewhere during the period of his contract, since the granting of an injunction is an equitable remedy and thus discretionary, and since the employee is only contracted on a part-time basis, it is unlikely that a court would be willing to comply in most cases. Perhaps if the contract reflected the need for particular fidelity, either through a specific express clause or in the level of salary paid, an injunction may be granted.

Garden leave

Although an order of specific performance may not be granted to oblige an employee to work for a particular employer (s.236 of the TULR(C)A 1992), in many cases companies are able to write long notice periods into contracts and then enforce the notice period without requiring the employee to actually attend for work. The effect of this is that the employee is paid to stay at home—"garden leave"—and may be legally restrained from taking up other employment during that notice period (*Evening Standard Co Ltd v Henderson* [1987] I.C.R. 588). Such clauses are now common in the contracts of senior employees, they enable an employer to protect all of their business interests for a period of several months should an employee decide to join a competitor.

In more recent years though the courts have adopted a less consistent approach to the issue of garden leave. Although in *GFI Group Inc v Eaglestone* [1994] I.R.L.R. 119 an injunction was granted prohibiting an employee from taking up new employment before his notice period had expired, in the case of *William Hill Org Ltd v Tucker* [1998] I.R.L.R. 313 the Court of Appeal both declined to grant a similar injunction and doubted that in such situations an injunction enforcing garden leave should be granted, but rather the employer should seek to rely upon a restrictive covenant within the employment contract.

Restrictive covenants

A restrictive covenant is an express term of the contract of employment which purports to extend beyond the life of the contract and restrain the employee from working, post contract, for a particular employer, in a particular industry, in a particular role, or in a particular location or geographical area, for an agreed length of time. Such terms are common in many employment contracts, their purpose being to prevent ex-employees from taking knowledge, skills, information, etc to a competitor.

However, the doctrine of restraint of trade holds that *prima facie* such agreements are void. The court will only uphold a restrictive covenant if it is satisfied that the employer has a legitimate proprietary interest to protect, such as a trade secret, a particular manufacturing process, a client base or, perhaps, its existing employees; and then only for as long as is fair and necessary.

In effect, the court has to balance the right of the ex-employee to work and do business, with the right of the ex-employer to reasonable protection. Whilst it is quite proper that confidential information and trade secrets of various types should be protected, it is equally proper that the individual should be permitted to practice and exercise skills and knowledge legitimately gained.

Illustrations from case law include:

(a) A promise not to use trade secrets or personal influence over customers may be enforced (*Spafax Ltd v Harrison* [1980] I.R.L.R. 442).

(b) Refusal by the employee to sign such an agreement may be a fair reason for dismissal (*RS Components v Irwin* [1973] I.C.R. 535).

(c) A promise not to use details of a secret manufacturing process for a period of five years was enforceable (*Forster & Sons Ltd v Suggett* (1918) 35 T.L.R. 87).

(d) A promise by an engineer not to work for a competitor for a period of seven years was not enforceable. It was held to be an unreasonable restriction on his knowledge and skill (*Herbert Morris Ltd v Saxelby* [1916] 1 A.C. 688).

(e) A promise by a negotiator in an estate agent's office not to work in that industry within a certain geographical area for a certain period of time was held not to be enforceable since the business was of a non-recurring type, and thus the agreement would not protect the employer's existing business, but merely restrain the employee from obtaining work (*Bowler v Lovegrove* [1921] 1 Ch. 642).

(f) An agreement preventing an employee from working within an industry or organisation in *any* capacity will generally be void as being wider than is necessary to protect a proprietary interest (*Littlewoods Organisation Ltd v Harris* [1978] 1 All E.R. 1026, *Commercial Plastics Ltd v Vincent* [1965] 1 Q.B. 623).

However:

(g) An agreement preventing an individual from working anywhere in the world, in a particular industry for a period of 25 years was held to be valid—since the promise had been bought for the equivalent of millions of pounds! (*Nordenfelt v Maxim Nordenfelt Guns Co Ltd* [1894] A.C. 535).

(h) An agreement preventing a solicitor's clerk from working for other solicitors within an area of a seven mile radius for the remainder of his life was held to be valid! (*Fitch v Dewes* [1921] 2 A.C. 158)—it is suggested that except in the most exceptional circumstances such an agreement would today be held to be far too wide to be enforceable.

The court will occasionally adopt a "blue pencil" approach to restraint of trade covenants, striking out such parts as are unenforceable, whilst upholding the remainder (*T Lucas & Co Ltd v Mitchell* [1974] Ch. 129). This is not the normal approach however, since the courts follow the contract doctrine of *contra proferentum*—in cases of doubt or ambiguity interpreting the clause against the party seeking to rely upon it.

CASE EXAMPLE

Faccenda Chicken Ltd v Fowler **[1986] I.C.R. 297**
Mr Fowler had worked for Faccenda as sales manager. He left and set up his own business in competition, employing several other Faccenda ex-employees. Between them they had information as to the names and addresses of Faccenda's customers, amounts of their orders and the prices charged. Faccenda argued that this was confidential information and Fowler should be restrained from using it.

Held:

> "It is clear that the obligation not to use or disclose information may cover secret processes . . . and other information which is of a sufficiently high degree of confidentiality as to amount to a trade secret.
> The obligation does not extend, however, to cover all information which is given to or acquired by the employee while in his employment, and in particular may not cover information which is only 'confidential' . . ."

Commentary: The judgment is worth reading in full for the distinctions it draws between "trade secrets" and other information, which whilst being "confidential", may not be protected once the employment is concluded.

15. TRADE UNIONS

A broad definition of a "trade union" is included in s.1 of the TULR(C)A 1992. It is an organisation of workers, or an association of such organisations, whose principal purposes include the regulation of relations between those workers and their employers. The courts have defined this definition strictly in such cases as *Midland Cold Storage v Turner* [1972] I.C.R. 773.

Section 10 of the TULR(C)A 1992 defines the status of a trade union as "quasi-corporate". As such, it is not a company, a provident society or a friendly society. It is, however, capable of:

(a) making contracts in its own name;
(b) suing and being sued in its own name; and
(c) having proceedings brought against it for offences committed by it or on its behalf.

Interestingly, and perhaps strangely, it would appear that a trade union may not however be able to bring an action for defamation in its own name (*EEPTU v Times Newspapers* [1980] 1 All E.R. 1097).

Independent Trade Union Status

It is necessary for a trade union to be granted independent status in order for it to gain various statutory rights: automatic employer recognition in certain circumstances; protection of its members against dismissal for union activities; time off for its members to undertake particular union activities; access to information for collective bargaining purposes, etc. An independent trade union is one which is not under the control of, or liable to interference from, an employer. The EAT in the case of *Blue Circle Staff Association v Certification Officer* [1977] 1 W.L.R. 239 laid down a list of guidelines for the Certification Officer when determining the status of a trade union; included in the list are such issues as whether the union is financially independent from the employer; whether the union rule book allows the employer to interfere with, or even control, the union; and whether the union has a "robust attitude in negotiation" with the employer. It is possible for a single-company union to obtain independent status, but both the courts and the Certification officer are likely to appreciate that such unions are more susceptible to influence from the employer than those unions operating over a range of employers.

Trade Union Recognition

Recognition of a trade union by the relevant employer is important. It entitles the union to involvement in collective bargaining activities; it may claim disclosure of information for such purposes; its representatives and members are entitled to time off for certain union activities; and the union must be consulted on training issues and opportunities. An employer may choose to recognise a union voluntarily, or under the ERelA 1999 there is automatic recognition by an employer of an independent trade union normally if either a majority of the workers in the bargaining unit are members of the trade union, or 40 per cent of those workers in the bargaining unit vote in favour of recognition. The process for recognition is supervised by the Central Arbitration Committee.

Trade Union Political Funds

If a trade union wishes to contribute towards political ends, such as contributions to political parties, that contribution must come from a separate political fund. This stems from the early days of the Labour Party, at which time Members of Parliament were unpaid, but Labour MPs received money from trade unions. The case of *ASRS v Osborne* [1910] A.C. 87 held that a levy on union members for political purposes was unlawful, but the Trade Union Act of 1913 subsequently allowed a union to set up a separate political fund into which union members could contribute if they wished. This is still the position today, although legislation has imposed restrictions on unions in terms of periodic ballots for maintaining such funds.

CASE EXAMPLE

Birch v National Union of Railwaymen **[1950] Ch. 602**
The NUR rulebook contained a rule that only those members contributing to the political fund may take part in the management of that fund. Mr Birch, who chose not to contribute to the political fund, was elected as a local branch official, part of

whose duties was an involvement in the management of the political fund. The union argued that he was not eligible for office, since he would be unable to fulfil all the required duties.

Held: The court held that the rule concerning the political fund offended against, what is now, s.82(1) of the TULR(C)A 1992. Whereas it was reasonable that only those members who contributed to the political fund should have authority to manage the fund, it was quite another thing that the rule should have the effect of disqualifying anyone not contributing to the fund from holding office of almost any sort within the union.

Commentary: The case is one of many examples demonstrating the involvement of the courts in the internal running of trade unions.

Freedom of Association

The right to freedom of association is contained in Art.11 of the ECHR. It includes the "right to freedom of association with others, including the right to form and join trade unions . . ." However, prior to 1988 in UK a "closed shop" principle was lawful—in order for a worker to get a job they must be a member of the trade union, should they leave the trade union they may not keep the job. This closed shop principle was outlawed by the Conservative government under Margaret Thatcher in a series of legislative measures during the 1980s. It should be noted that there are some statutory restrictions concerning the ability of certain groups to either join a trade union or to take part in industrial action; police officers are not permitted to join a trade union, although they are automatically members of the Police Federation; members of the armed forces are not permitted to take part in industrial action; members of the security services have a clause in their contracts of employment by which they agree not to join a trade union; and certain Crown employees have similar exclusions.

CASE EXAMPLE

Young, James and Webster v United Kingdom **[1981] I.R.L.R. 408 ECHR**
At the time, British Rail operated a closed shop. Employment within British Rail at many levels was only permitted if the employee joined the appropriate trade union; should he refuse to join or subsequently leave the union, his employment would terminate. The three complainants had all refused to join the trade union and had been dismissed by British Rail. They took their case to the ECHR.

Held: The court held that the right to form or join a trade union is a fundamental aspect of freedom of association. Conversely, therefore, the right not to join or to leave a union must also form part of the basic right of freedom of association. The actions of British Rail supported by domestic legislation in UK therefore breached Art.11 of the Convention.

Commentary: It must be remembered that the closed shop principle is no longer lawful in the UK, and also that this case was heard long before the judgments of the ECHR had effect in UK courts or legislation.

Union Rules

The union rules will form part of the contract between the union and its members. As such, both the union rules and disciplinary procedures are open to scrutiny by the courts (*Lee v The Showmen's Guild of Great Britain* [1952] 2 Q.B. 329) and are subject to issues of natural justice (*Roebuck v National Union of Mineworkers (Yorkshire Area) No 2* [1978] I.C.R. 676). All individual union members have the right not to be unjustifiably disciplined by the trade union (s.64 of the TULR(C)A 1992). Any union member complaining of unjustified action by the union may present a complaint within three months to an Employment Tribunal.

16. INDUSTRIAL ACTION

At common law, all industrial action will amount to a breach of the contract of employment. A strike—withdrawal of labour—will obviously constitute a breach of contract (*Simmons v Hoover Ltd* [1977] I.C.R. 61, as will a work to rule (*Secretary of State for Employment v ASLEF* [1972] 2 All E.R. 949, or indeed a refusal to work non-contractual overtime (*Faust v Power Packing Casemakers Ltd* [1983] I.R.L.R. 117). However, statute has intervened to offer an amount of protection to trade unions and their members in certain situations.

Official and Unofficial Action

It is important to distinguish between official and unofficial industrial action. Official action is that which is supported by the trade union; unofficial action is that which the union has not repudiated. For action to be deemed unofficial it is not sufficient that the union merely does not support it; the union must actively repudiate the action (*Express and Star Ltd v NGA* [1985] I.R.L.R. 455) by giving immediate notice of repudiation to those organising the action (s.21(2)(a) of the TULR(C)A 1992) and to all union members and their employers who may become involved in the action (s.21(2)(b) of the TULR(C)A 1992).

One reason for differentiating between official and unofficial action is that if workers are dismissed for taking part in unofficial action the employment tribunal will have no jurisdiction to hear their complaint of unfair dismissal.

The position regarding unfair dismissal for taking part in industrial action is governed by ss.237–239 of the TULR(C)A 1992.

Dismissal for participation in unofficial action is effectively automatically fair (s.237).

Dismissal for participation in lawful official action is automatically unfair. This protection lasts for eight weeks from the start of the official action (or longer if the employer has failed to take reasonable procedural steps to resolve the dispute, s.238A(6) of the TULR(C)A 1992), after which time the dismissal will be fair, subject to s.238A of the TULR(C)A 1992.

Dismissal for participation in official action which is unlawful, or has lasted over eight weeks at the time of dismissal, is automatically fair, unless:

(i) not all current participants in the action have been dismissed; or

(ii) within three months of the dismissals, some or any (but not all) of those dismissed are selectively re-employed. In such cases the employment tribunal would consider the issue of fairness of dismissal by applying the "reasonableness" test.

Trade Unions' Liability in Tort

The structure of the law in this area is very complex. Perhaps the simplest way of tackling a problem question in this issue it is to adopt a three-stage approach:

(a) Has a tort been committed?
(b) If so, is the action protected by the immunity granted by s.219 of the TULR(C)A 1992?
(c) If so, has the immunity been lost by the union's failure to comply with legislation (mainly ss.222–226 of the TULR(C)A) 1992?

Has a Tort been committed? It is important to identify which torts may have been committed during industrial action. The commission of some torts—the major economic torts—may in some circumstances be granted immunity by statute, but the organisers of industrial action, usually the trade union, will still have liability for torts such as public nuisance (*News Group Newspapers Ltd v SOGAT '82* [1986] I.R.L.R. 337).

The Major Economic Torts

The scope of these economic torts has been increased over the years by the courts; the major torts are: inducement to breach of contract; interference with contract; interference with trade or business; intimidation; and conspiracy.

Inducement to Breach of Contract. This tort can take two forms, direct or indirect.

The direct form occurs when an inducement is made by one party, usually the trade union, to the second party, the employee, to breach a contract which the second party has with the third party, the employer. Generally the contract is the employee's contract of employment, and the breach may be a withdrawal of labour—a strike—(*Simmons v Hoover Ltd* [1977] I.C.R. 61), a "go-slow" or work to rule (*British Telecommunications Plc v Ticehurst* [1992] I.C.R. 383) or other form of industrial action (*Wiluszynski v Tower Hamlets LBC* [1989] I.C.R. 493). The generally quoted example of a direct inducement to breach of contract is the old case of *Lumley v Gye* [1853] 2 E & B 216, in which an opera singer who was under contract to appear at a particular theatre was persuaded by an agent to break her contract and appear instead at a different theatre. The agent was liable for, what was then, the new tort of inducement to breach of contract.

The indirect form of the tort is slightly more complicated. It requires that party A should induce party B to cause a breach of a contract between parties C and D. An example is the case of *DC Thomson & Co Ltd v Deakin* [1952] Ch. 646, in which the trade union called upon workers in several companies to refuse to handle deliveries to a particular company, DC Thomson, who were in dispute with the union. Workers from another company, Bowaters, made it clear to their employer that they would not handle deliveries to Thomson's. Thomson's then sought action against the trade union for the tort of inducement to breach of contract. The court held that the tort would be committed if the following four elements were proved:

(a) if the trade union knew of the existence of the contract and intended its breach;
(b) if the union did induce a breach of the contract;
(c) if the employees so persuaded did indeed breach their contracts of employment; and
(d) if the breach of their contracts of employment did cause the breach of the contract complained of.

The later case of *Emerald Construction Ltd v Lowthian* [1966] 1 W.L.R. 691 makes it clear that it is not necessary that the union should have any detailed knowledge of the contract, merely that it is aware, or should be aware, in general terms, of the existence of such a contract.

It is said that for the indirect form of the tort of inducement to breach of contract "unlawful means" must be used. These unlawful means need be nothing more than another tort themselves. In the case of *DC Thomson* the unlawful means would be the inducement to the workers to breach their contracts of employment—itself the simple or direct form of the tort. To prove the direct form of this tort no unlawful means are necessary. It should be noted that if the "unlawful means" are themselves protected by the immunities under s.219 of the TULR(C)A 1992, they will not constitute unlawful means for the purpose of this tort (see the section on "immunities").

Interference with Contract. This is essentially an extended version of the tort of inducement to breach of contract. The important difference is that it is not necessary to prove an actual breach of a contract. According to Lord Denning in the case of *Torquay Hotel Co Ltd v Cousins* [1969] 2 Ch. 106 if a person deliberately interferes with the trade or business of another by any means which are unlawful, then a tort will be committed, even though no actual breach of contract may arise.

Interference with Trade or Business. This may be viewed as either a further extension of the torts of inducement to breach of contract and interference with contract, or an "umbrella" tort of which the two previous torts are merely sub-species. Its existence was confirmed by the House of Lords in *Merkur Island Shipping Corp v Laughton* [1983] 2 All E.R. 189, where it was stated that there was no need to prove interference with any particular or specific contract, thus confirming Lord Denning's dicta in *Torquay Hotel* (above). It would therefore be possible to commit this tort by frightening off potential, rather than actual, customers. As with the tort of interference with contract, however, it must be shown that unlawful means have been employed, which in practice will usually simply mean that the commission of this tort has involved the commission of another tort.

Intimidation. Although the courts have long held that the threat of physical violence may constitute an unlawful act, usually a criminal act, it was not until the case of *Rookes v Barnard* [1964] A.C. 1129 that the tort of intimidation was identified through the use of threats of breach of contract. Lord Devlin stated in that case: "I find nothing to differentiate a threat of a breach of contract from a threat of physical violence or other illegal threat." Thus putting pressure on an employer to act in a certain way by threatening to breach a contract, often the contract of employment, will amount to the commission of the tort of intimidation.

Conspiracy. If two or more combine to injure another, and their predominant purpose is to injure the other rather than to advance their own legitimate interests, the tort of conspiracy will be committed. This form of the tort has little practical importance following the case of *Crofter Hand Woven Harris Tweed Co v Veitch* [1942] A.C. 435, where it was accepted by the House of Lords that normal trade union purposes were "legitimate interests" as long as they were the predominant motive of the organisers of the industrial action. However, if "unlawful means" are used the defence of legitimate interests will not succeed; it is not clear whether a simple breach of contract would be sufficient to constitute unlawful means for the commission of this tort.

Is the Action Protected by an Immunity?

The Statutory Immunities

Section 219 of the TULR(C)A 1992 provides, to at least some extent, immunity from liability in the commission of all of the above torts. This immunity will only apply where the actions complained of are carried out **"in contemplation and furtherance of a trade dispute"**—the so-called "Golden Formula".
Section 219(1) of the TULR(C)A 1992 states:

"An act done by a person in contemplation or furtherance of a trade dispute is not actionable in tort on the ground only—
  (a) that it induces another person to break a contract or interferes or induces another person to interfere with its performance, or
    [thus protecting directly against Inducement of Breach of Contract and Interference with Contract and indirectly against Interference with Business by limiting the scope for 'unlawful means']
  (b) that it consists in his threatening that a contract (whether one to which he is a party or not) will be broken or its performance interfered with, or that he will induce another person to break a contract or interfere with its performance.
    [thus protecting directly against Intimidation and indirectly against Inducement of Breach of Contract, Interference with Contract and Interference with Business by limiting the scope for 'unlawful means']"

Section 219(2) states:

"An agreement or combination by two or more persons to do or procure the doing of an act in contemplation or furtherance of a trade dispute is not actionable in tort if the act is one which if done without any such agreement or combination would not be actionable in tort.

[thus protecting directly against conspiracy to injure without the use of unlawful means and also conspiracy to use unlawful means **except** where it is an agreement to commit a tort]".

The Golden Formula

Protection under s.219 is only granted to those actions which are carried out in contemplation or furtherance of a trade dispute.

A trade dispute is defined in s.244 of the TULR(C)A 1992 as a dispute between workers and their employer which relates wholly or mainly to such issues as terms and conditions of employment.

It would thus exclude disputes where the union is motivated mainly by "political" considerations, *e.g.* ideological objections to privatisation (*Mercury Communications Ltd v Scott-Garner* [1984] I.C.R. 741) or refusing to handle mail for South Africa as an anti-apartheid protest (*Gouriet v UPOW* [1978] A.C. 435), as well as disputes motivated mainly by personal spite (*Torquay Hotels Ltd v Cousins* [1969] 2 Ch. 106; *Huntley v Thornton* [1957] 1 All E.R. 234).

"In Contemplation" requires the dispute to be imminent— *Bent's Brewery Co Ltd v Hogan* [1945] 2 All E.R. 570.

"In Furtherance" presupposes a dispute already in existence and not yet over (see, *e.g. Stewart v AUEW* [1973] I.C.R. 128). An action is in furtherance of the dispute if D genuinely believes it will further its interests in the dispute whether or not it will or is capable of doing so and whether or not it is a reasonable means of doing so (*Express Newspapers Ltd v McShane* [1980] I.C.R. 42; *NWL Ltd v Woods* [1979] 1 W.L.R. 1294).

Has the Immunity been Lost? The statutory immunities contained in s.219 of the TULR(C)A 1992 will be lost if any of the requirements contained in the legislation, mainly in ss.222–234 of the TULR(C)A 1992, are breached. This covers such issues as:

(a) taking action to enforce union membership (s.222 of the TULR(C)A 1992);

(b) taking action due to the dismissal of an employee for taking unofficial industrial action (s.223 of the TULR(C)A 1992);

(c) if the action amounts to secondary action (s.224 of the TULR(C)A 1992);

(d) if the action is to impose union recognition (s.225 of the TULR(C)A 1992); or

(e) if the extensive requirements concerning the organisation of the ballot have not been met (ss.226–234 of the TULR(C)A 1992).

If the immunities have been lost, or if torts have been committed which are not covered by the protection afforded by s.219 of the TULR(C)A 1992, the trade union may be liable for damages in a civil action for tort.

Picketing

Section 220 of the TULR(C)A 1992 states:

> "It is lawful for a person in contemplation or furtherance of a trade dispute to attend—(a) at or near his own place of work, or (b) if he is an official of a trade union, at or near the place of work of a member of the union whom he is accompanying and whom he represents, for the purpose only of peacefully obtaining or communicating information, or peacefully persuading any person to work or abstain from working."

It should therefore be noted that:

(a) the picketing must come within the Golden Formula;

(b) the picketing must be at or near the pickets' workplace— in the case of *Rayware Ltd v TGWU* [1989] I.R.L.R. 134 the Court of Appeal held that this should be the closest point to their workplace at which the pickets could lawfully assemble;

(c) picketing is for clearly defined purposes only—in the case of *Broome v DPP* [1974] I.C.R. 84 a picket was arrested for attempting to stop a vehicle entering his employer's premises; and

(d) picketing must be peaceful—a large number of pickets could not be said to be "peacefully communicating", their purpose was to intimidate (*Thomas v NUM* [1985] I.R.L.R. 136), in which the court restricted picket numbers to a maximum of six.

Employer's Remedies against individual employee participants

Apart from any remedy the employer may have against the trade union—generally either injunction or action in tort for damages—the employer may also have remedies against the individual employee:

(a) The courts will not grant the remedy of specific performance against an employee (s.236 of the TULR(C)A 1992).

(b) Damages may be awarded, but only for the individual's own contribution to the loss, so such a remedy is not usually sought in practice (*NCB v Galley* [1958] 1 W.L.R. 16).

(c) Deductions from wages, amounting in effect to self-assessed damages and permitted under s.14(5) of the ERA 1996, see, *e.g. Miles v Wakefield MDC* [1987] I.C.R. 368 and *Wiluszynski v London Borough of Tower Hamlets* [1989] I.C.R. 493.

(d) Dismissal at common law may be contractually permitted without notice where, as will usually be the case, the employee's action is a repudiatory breach. However, whether or not the action is in breach of contract, the position concerning unfair dismissal is governed by ss.237–239 of the TULR(C)A 1992 which distinguish between official (*i.e.* backed by his trade union) and unofficial action.

Dismissal for participation in unofficial action is effectively automatically fair (s.237 of the TULR(C)A 1992).

Dismissal for participation in official action which is lawful, *i.e.* non-tortious, is automatically unfair. This protection lasts for eight weeks from the start of the official action (or longer if the employer has failed to take reasonable procedural steps to resolve the dispute—see s.238A(6) of the TULR(C)A 1992) after which the dismissal will be fair subject to the next provision (s.238A of the TULR(C)A 1992).

Dismissal for participation in official action which is unlawful (or has lasted over eight weeks at time of dismissal) is automatically fair unless:

(i) not all current participants have been dismissed; or

(ii) within three months of the claimant's dismissal, one or more dismissed participants has been offered re-engagement when the claimant has not (s.238 of the

TULR(C)A 1992). In such a case, the Employment
Tribunal must consider whether the dismissal was
fair or unfair using the standard "reasonableness"
test.

17. EXAMINATION CHECKLIST

1. Why is it necessary to distinguish between a contract of
    service and a contract for services?
2. How do the courts distinguish between an employee and
    an independent contractor?
3. What is the legal status of a section 1 statement?
4. How may the products of a collective agreement become a
    term of an individual's contract of employment?
5. Does an employer have to act "reasonably" when enforc-
    ing a contractual term?
6. What is the relationship between the Duty of Mutual Trust
    and Confidence and other contractual terms?
7. What are the three heads of claim for equal pay?
8. Who makes the choice of comparator in an equal pay
    claim?
9. What is the role of the Independent Expert in an equal pay
    claim?
10. What is meant by "leap-frogging" in equal pay?
11. What forms of discrimination are unlawful?
12. What is the difference between "direct" and "indirect"
    discrimination?
13. Why was discrimination against part-time workers
    declared unlawful?
14. Is "positive discrimination" unlawful?
15. Is discrimination on the grounds of sexual orientation
    unlawful? Does this differ from discrimination against
    transsexuals?
16. When may an employer be liable for the discriminatory
    acts of his employees?
17. What is meant by the "duty to make adjustments" in terms
    of Disability Discrimination?

18. To whom does the National Minimum Wage Act apply?
19. Is it possible for all workers to opt out of all aspects of the Working Time Regulations?
20. Is dismissal on the grounds of pregnancy always unfair?
21. Is dismissal on the grounds of pregnancy related illness unfair?
22. How may a disclosure become a "protected disclosure" under the Public Interest Disclosure Act?
23. What is the difference between "contributory negligence" and *"volenti non fit injuria"*?
24. How does an employer's vicarious liability in Health and Safety differ from vicarious liability in Discrimination?
25. What is the difference between "wrongful dismissal" and "unfair dismissal"?
26. What is meant by "continuity of employment"? Do all periods of unemployment break continuity?
27. What are the potentially fair reasons for dismissal?
28. Can dismissal for a fair reason be an unfair dismissal?
29. What is meant by "statutory dispute resolution procedure"?
30. What is the importance of the ACAS Code of Practice?
31. What are the remedies for unfair dismissal?
32. How have the courts defined "work of a particular kind" with regard to redundancy?
33. What is the importance of the procedure laid down in *Williams v Compair Maxam*?
34. What is meant by a "transfer of undertakings"?
35. What is meant by "garden leave"?
36. What is the balance the courts seek to strike before upholding a restrictive covenant?
37. What is meant by "an independent trade union"?
38. Do the courts have jurisdiction to interfere with a trade union's rule book?
39. Differentiate between official and unofficial industrial action.
40. What are the major economic torts?
41. What is meant by "the golden formula"?
42. Is picketing lawful?

18. EXAMINATION GUIDANCE QUESTIONS

Examination questions in employment law usually take one of two forms—either essay questions or problem questions. These are very different, both in format and in what is required of the examinee, and we will look at each type of question in turn.

Students usually prefer one type of question to the other, the majority normally opting for the problem question. Unfortunately for many students, examinations are usually set in a way that requires the student to attempt at least one of each style of question.

Very few, if any, questions ever require the student to write all he or she knows about a topic, and it is very possible for even the most knowledgeable student to make a poor showing in an examination by simply not answering the question that has been asked. Fortunately, answering examination questions is a skill, and like any other skill, it may be learned.

Before going into the examination room you will probably know both how long the examination lasts and how many questions you are required to answer; if so, work out in advance how much time you can afford to spend on each question—and stick to it! The first 20 per cent or 30 per cent of marks are the easiest to get and are normally obtainable in the first few minutes of your answer, after that, marks become progressively more difficult to obtain; so don't be tempted to spend half of your time on the first of three questions and find yourself with no time for the third! Don't forget to allow for several minutes reading time, ideally both at the start and at the end of the examination.

Many examinations allow you to take an unannotated statute book into the examination room. Make full use of this by ensuring that you are familiar with the layout and format of the book beforehand—specific statute referencing may gain you several marks, and in some questions, *e.g.* redundancy, statute should be your starting point.

Once inside the examination room the most basic rule to remember when presented with an examination paper is that putting pen to paper is one of the last things you should do!

The following format may help:

(a) Read through the paper. Pay particular attention to the instructions.

(b) Read through the paper again, deciding which questions to answer, and perhaps making brief preliminary notes.

(c) Prepare an answer plan. Read through the answer plan ensuring that it answers the question asked.

(d) Write your answer, supporting each proposition with an authority of either statute or case law.

(e) Read through your answer, making sure that what you are reading is what you have written, and that what you have written is what you meant to write.

(f) If you have time remaining, re-read both the question and answer—just to be on the safe side!

(g) Finally, an obvious point: if you do start to run out of time, answer in note form—do not simply give up, it is surprising how many relevant points you can make in just five minutes writing time.

ESSAY QUESTIONS

Although most students seem to prefer problem questions to essay questions, a well answered essay question is probably more likely to gain better marks than a well answered problem. The advantage to an essay question, assuming you have a good knowledge of your subject, is that you are not as constrained by the question and you have more opportunity to develop ideas and approaches. However, the same rules apply to both types of question: support your arguments with authorities and ensure that you understand what the question requires of you.

If you are not confident in the topic, or if you are not sure what is required by the examiner, you would be well advised not to attempt that essay question.

Style of writing, and, to some extent, the structure of your answer are personal matters. Trying to imitate another's style is unlikely to be successful, and whilst it is all very well to say that an essay should have a start, a middle and an end, not all essay questions lend themselves to that treatment.

What is important—apart from content, which is essential—is ensuring that you write legibly, with decent grammar and reasonable spelling, so that the examiner can not only read what you have written, but can also understand what you mean.

As with all examination questions, it is very important that you re-read what you have written. Do not make the mistake once you have finished the exam of staring out of the window or leaving early—use any time remaining to re-read and re-check.

PROBLEM QUESTIONS

The advantage to a problem question is that you are given much more information in the question on which to base your answer. Assuming you understand what the question requires of you, and you have knowledge of the topic, the main problem is how to structure your answer. The two important factors are:

(a) a good answer plan; and
(b) plenty of practice.

Question 1

Adam is an insurance salesman with XCo Ltd. He has been an employee for over three years. He spends most of his time either working from home using a computer terminal supplied by the company, and visiting customers, using his own car, for which he is paid an allowance. On average Adam spends no more than half a day per week in the company's offices.

The company have recently suggested to Adam that he change his status from employee to self-employed, as they believe this will result in financial benefit to both parties.

Advise Adam.

Suggested points for consideration A genuine change of Adam's status from employee to self-employed may well benefit both parties financially:

For Adam it would mean that he may offset various expenses against tax payable, almost certainly showing a financial benefit. However, he will lose many of the rights of an employee, *e.g.* redundancy payments, right to complain of unfair dismissal,etc.

For the company, not only will there be financial savings on payrolling and employer's National Insurance contributions, etc., but their liability will be considerably decreased in many situations: no employer's vicarious liability; reduced standard of care in many situations; many employee's rights will not apply, *e.g.* redundancy, unfair dismissal, etc.

Would the courts accept such a change of status?

Consider the "multiple test" (*Ready Mix Concrete*).

Is Adam in business on his own account? (*Market Investigations*).

Self-description (*Ferguson cf. Massey*).

Reason for the court's involvement (*Lorimer cf. Lane*).

Question 2

Brian has worked for XCo Ltd for five years as an accounts clerk, operating a manual system of accounts. Last week the company announced that it was computerising its accounts system, and all the accounts clerks would need to undergo training in order to adapt to the new system. XCo Ltd intend running a training course of one hour after work on Tuesdays and Fridays for the next month, for which the employees will be paid overtime rates.

Brian is unhappy; he does not understand computers and at 55 years old believes he is too old to learn. Also Friday is Brian's darts night, and he has previously made it clear that he is not prepared to work late on Fridays—XCo Ltd have never before insisted that he should. Finally, Brian maintains that he is not employed to operate a computer and XCo Ltd have no right to insist that he should.

Advise Brian.

Suggested points for consideration. Common sense suggests from the facts that Brian, having had no experience of computers, is simply afraid of them, and a sensible and reassuring talk with either his manager or the personnel manager may resolve the problem.

Brian should be advised that although generally the company may not make unilateral changes to the contract of employment, they do have every right to update their procedures, particularly for "sound good business reasons" (*Hollister v NFU*), and if, as in this case, they provide training, the employee has a duty to adapt (*Cresswell*). In this case there may be a question as to whether the company have given sufficient notice of the change (*United Bank*), but on the facts given it is unlikely that such an argument would succeed. It is also unlikely that a tribunal would have much sympathy for Brian's darts night; were the issue to become one of unfair dismissal, the court would consider the conduct of the employer, rather than the effect on the employee, when deciding the fairness of the issue (*Devis v Atkins*).

Is there any strength in Brian's implied argument that this is a change of job rather than merely a change in method of performing the existing job (*Butterwick*)?

Question 3

Clive has worked as a laboratory technician for XCo Ltd since 1987 at their Manchester works.

In January 1990 Clive was sent a revised statement of terms and conditions which contained among other things the following clause: "The company reserves the right to transfer any employee either temporarily or permanently to any of the company's business premises anywhere within the UK." As requested, Clive signed and returned the bottom copy of the document to the personnel office.

Last week Clive was informed by the personnel manager that owing to a downturn in work at the Manchester offices Clive would be transferred next month to the Birmingham branch.

Clive complained that this would entail either relocation or considerable daily travel, neither of which was acceptable.

The personnel manager referred Clive to the mobility clause, and told him: "You have no option; work in Birmingham or resign."

Advise Clive.

Suggested points for consideration. In advising Clive, the first thing to consider is whether the mobility clause contained in the January 1990 statement forms part of his contract of employment (*Gascol Conversions*). If it does, then the company has every contractual right to enforce it (*Western Excavating*), as long as it is not invoked in such a way so as to breach the duty of mutual trust and confidence (*United Bank*). Consider, perhaps, whether cases such as *High Table v Horst* may be of assistance to Clive.

If the mobility clause does not form part of the employment contract, the company would have to rely on an implied mobility clause under the terms of mutual trust and confidence and the employee's duty of co-operation, but it is very unlikely on the facts of Clive's case that such an argument would succeed (*Aparau v Iceland Frozen Foods*).

The other issue here concerns the words used by the personnel manager. If Clive leaves the company, has there been a dismissal, which there must be for a successful redundancy or unfair dismissal claim. Is this a case of resignation under the threat of dismissal (*Sussex CC v Walker*) or would the employer's actions constitute a repudiatory breach of the contract in which case s.95(1)(c) of the ERA 1996 would apply?

Question 4

David and Emily are employed as machine operators by XCo. David has worked for them for one and a half years, and Emily for eight months.

Emily discovers that David earns £6.00 per hour, whereas she is only paid £5.50 per hour. She also discovers that fork-lift truck drivers employed by a subsidiary of XCo in London are paid £8.00 per hour.

Advise XCo of the defences that may be available to them should Emily bring an equal pay claim.

Suggested points for consideration. Emily may bring two possible claims:

(a) A claim under like work (s.1(2)(a) of the EqPA 1970), using David as her comparator; or
(b) A claim for work of equal value (s.1(2)(c) of the EqPA 1970), using the fork-lift operators as comparators.

The choice of comparators is for Emily to make (*Pickstone*), and she may choose multiple comparators if she wishes (*Hayward v Cammell Laird*).

Defences available to the company under a like work claim may include:

(a) David has been employed for over twice as long as Emily, the pay difference may be justified if the company can show that it is part of a recognised pay structure that is not based on the sex of the employee (s.1(3) of the EqPA 1970).
(b) If the company can show that David's pay has been "red circled" (*Snoxell*).
(c) If there are genuine material differences between the work that David and Emily actually do (*Shields v Coombes*).

Factors which may defeat a claim for work of equal value include:

(a) If the fork lift operators are women Emily may not use them as comparators.
(b) If the work of the fork lift operators is not of equal value to Emily's.
(c) If common terms and conditions are not observed between XCo and their subsidiary (*Leverton*).
(d) If the differential is due to different geographical locations (*NAAFI v Varley*).

Question 5

Felicity is 34 years old, a single mother with two young children, and has just started work for XCo Ltd on their production line. On her first morning she sees the production manager point at her and ask the line supervisor: "Who's the new tart with the big knockers?"

Felicity is very upset by this remark, which she believes was overheard by several other workers; she goes to see the personnel manager to complain. He tells her "not to be a silly girl" and to return to work.

Advise Felicity.

Would your advice be different if Felicity also worked part time as an "exotic dancer" at the Blue Parrot Strip Club?

Suggested points for consideration. The question raises several issues:

(a) Even one remark, if sufficiently serious, can amount to sexual harassment (*In Situ Cleaning*), even if they were not addressed to Felicity (*De Souza v AA*).

(b) The company may be held vicariously liable for the actions of its employees, even if they were not sanctioned (*Porcelli*), if the actions were committed in the course of employment (*Jones v Tower Boot*).

(c) Despite dicta to the contrary in *De Souza*, later case law suggests that the harassment itself constitutes the "detriment" necessary under s.6(2)(b) of the SDA 1975 (*In Situ Cleaning*).

(d) It is an implied term of the employment contract that it should have and operate an effective grievance procedure (*WA Goold (Pearmak) Ltd*), and in particular, failure by an employer to take seriously a complaint of sexual or racial discrimination will count heavily against the company (*In Situ Cleaning*).

Felicity may therefore be advised that she may have grounds to bring a complaint of direct sex discrimination against her employer, for which there is no requirement of any qualifying period of employment.

The relevance of Felicity being a part time exotic dancer is that the tribunal may take this and other details of the applicant's background and lifestyle into account when assessing the level of detriment suffered by her (*Wileman v Minilec Engg*) prior to awarding compensation.

Question 6

Gertrude has been employed as an invoice clerk by XCo Ltd for the past five years. In previous years all the staff in her department have received annual pay increases including Gertrude, but this year she discovers that she is the only person not to receive a rise.

When Gertrude sees the personnel manager to ask why, she is told: "Your work is not up to standard. Why don't you just take the hint and resign?"

Gertrude is very upset, she says the comment is very unfair and she cannot accept it.

Gertrude continues to work at XCo until last week, when she announced her immediate resignation and walked out.

Advise XCo Ltd of their legal position in relation to her departure from the company.

Suggested points for consideration. The question concerns the issue of constructive dismissal. Have either the actions of the company in failing to award Gertrude a pay rise, or the words of the personnel manager, amounted to a repudiation by the company of the contract, which would allow Gertrude to leave and claim constructive dismissal?

Unless an employee has a term in the employment contract to the contrary, there is no implied term that pay increases will be awarded (*Murco Petroleum v Forge*); although if an employer acts capriciously in witholding a pay increase that may amount to a breach of the implied term of mutual trust and confidence (*United Bank v Akhtar*, and *obiter* in *Murco*).

The words used by the personnel manager may constitute a breach of the term of mutual trust and confidence. That would be a question of fact for the tribunal, who would consider such factors as the relationship between the parties, any prior history, etc. (*Isle of Wight Tourist Board v Coombes*).

By continuing to work Gertrude may have affirmed the contract, much would depend upon how much time elapsed between the incident and her leaving, and also upon whether she had made it clear that she did not accept the situation (*Marriott v Oxford Co-op*).

Remember that following the EA 2002, both parties should follow the statutory dispute resolution procedure.

Question 7

Harry and Ian both worked for XCo Ltd in their warehouse. It was common knowledge that they did not get on with each other, and on one occasion the personnel manager had given both of them a "first and final warning", when an argument between them had resulted in an angry exchange, threats and an amount of "pushing and shoving".

Yesterday afternoon the personnel manager called both of them into his office following complaints from another worker that "it sounds as if they are killing each other in there!"

Harry had a cut lip and a bruised hand, Ian had a black eye. When questioned, both were sullen; Harry mumbled "he started it", whereas Ian claimed he had walked into a door.

The personnel manager told them that fighting constituted gross misconduct, and in any case they had both had a previous warning; consequently both were summarily dismissed and must leave the premises immediately.

Discuss any likely action by Harry and/or Ian.

Suggested points for consideration. The two courses of action open to Harry and Ian would be actions for either unfair dismissal or wrongful dismissal.

Unfair dismissal

  (a) Can the applicant claim? Both would appear to be employees. Neither belong to an excluded group. Although we are not told, it may be assumed that both have a minimum of one year's service. The claim must be brought within three months.
  (b) Can a dismissal be identified? Yes—both have been summarily dismissed.
  (c) The reason for the dismissal. The reason for the dismissal is the conduct of the employees, *i.e.* fighting. "Conduct" is a potentially fair reason for dismissal under s.98(2)(b) of the ERA 1996.
  (d) The fairness of the dismissal.
      (i) Did the actions of the employer fall within the band of reasonable responses which a reasonable employer might have adopted (*Iceland Frozen Foods v Jones*)? In this case, dismissal of employees for fighting may well amount to a reasonable response.

(ii) Procedural fairness (*Polkey v Dayton*) and, more importantly, the statutory dispute resolution procedure once it is implemented under the EA 2002 (expected to be Summer/Autumn 2003).

It may be helpful to apply the test from *BHS v Burchell*:

(1) that the employer honestly held the belief;
(2) that the employer had reasonable grounds on which to sustain that belief; and
(3) that the employer had carried out a reasonable investigation.

In this case, the test is probably satisfied. The employer believed that the employees had been fighting, there were reasonable grounds for that belief, and since it appears that there were no witnesses, it is difficult to know what further investigation could have been made.

However, one important issue remains; is a *summary* dismissal justified in the circumstances? This would depend on several factors, is there a contract term stating that fighting constitutes gross misconduct, what were the specific terms of the warning given, when was the warning given, how has the company reacted to other instances of fighting?

Wrongful dismissal

An action for wrongful dismissal generally concerns only whether the correct contract notice period has been given (*Addis*) and not the reason for the dismissal as such. In this case the tribunal would need to decide whether the company were contractually entitled to dismiss the employees without notice (*Sinclair v Neighbour*).

Question 8

Advise XCo in the following situations:

(a) The company wishes to dismiss John, one of their warehouse operatives, who has just been sentenced to six months' imprisonment.
(b) The company is concerned that Keith and Larry, delivery drivers, are working during their holidays for one of XCo's competitors, and may pass on trade secrets.

Suggested points for consideration

(a) Regarding John, the company would appear to have two options. Firstly, they may dismiss him on the grounds either of "conduct" or "some other substantial reason". The tribunal may take into account such factors as whether John's conduct occurred inside or outside of his employment, whether his conduct has a bearing on his ability to do his job, etc., but there is plenty of case law to suggest that the dismissal would be held to be fair, *e.g. Mathewson v RB Wilson Dental Laboratories*, particularly if the company act within the ACAS code of practice.

The company's second option would be to declare that John's term of imprisonment has frustrated the contract (*Shepherd v Jerrom*), and thus the contract is automatically terminated without a dismissal taking place. Again, the tribunal would consider such factors as length of sentence, need for the employee's work to be done, availability of a replacement, etc.

(b) Regarding Keith and Larry, the court must balance a reluctance to restrict the ability of individuals to increase their earnings through spare time working, with the right of a company to protect its legitimate interests (*Hivac v Park Royal Scientific*). The company may either attempt to obtain an injunction to prevent its employees being employed elsewhere during the existence of their contract of employment, or it may wish to dismiss the employees, claiming that they are in breach of faith. However, be aware of such case law as *Nova Plastics v Froggatt*, in which the dismissal of an odd-job man for part time working with a competitor was held to be unfair, in view of the fact that due to his position he was hardly likely to cause any harm to his employers.

Question 9

Maureen has been employed by XCo for just over two years, working in the sales department. The previous holder of the post, Nora, has been with the company for over 20 years and is now in the customer services department. The company has just announced that due to a shortage of new orders the customer services department is being closed, Nora is being transferred back to the sales department, and Maureen is being made redundant at the end of the month.

Advise Maureen of any claim she may have against XCo.

Suggested points for consideration. The question concerns redundancy, and in particular the practice known as "bumping". The starting point for any answer should be s.139(1) of the ERA 1996, followed by consideration of the three tests applied by the courts: the contract test, the job function test, and the statutory test. Of particular relevance is the test from *Safeway v Burrell*, which allows for the principle of "bumping" and this is supported by *Murray v Foyle Meats*.

Assuming that the company follows a similar procedure to that laid down in *Williams v Compair*, application of *Safeway* would suggest that Maureen has no claim against redundancy.

Question 10

Mrs Oswald has worked for XCo since 1993. She worked from home filling envelopes, on average working some 20 hours per week. Some weeks there was almost no work for her, in others she worked over 40 hours. The company have always treated her as self-employed, paying her gross, and not providing holiday or sick pay.

Two months ago XCo sold its business as a going concern to YCo Ltd, who have a policy of not using home workers. Consequently, for the past two months Mrs Oswald has received no work.

Advise Mrs Oswald.

Suggested points for consideration. If Mrs Oswald is self-employed she will have no claim against either XCo or YCo. However, if she is an employee, under TUPE 1981 her dismissal by YCo is automatically unfair, although the company may have a defence under ETO reasons. Alternatively, the failure to provide her with an opportunity to earn wages would amount to a breach of contract (*Devonald v Rosser*).

To determine Mrs Oswald's status apply dicta from *Nethermere v Gardiner* and *Carmichael v National Power*, and have particular note of the ERA 1999 which permits the granting of employment rights to various groups, including home workers.

INDEX